Your Church Helping People Be Like Jesus

TRANSFORMATIONAL DISCIPLESHIP

Barry Sneed & Roy Edgemon

LifeWay Press
Nashville, Tennessee

ISBN 0-7673-9847-5

Dewey Decimal Classification: 268

Subject Heading: Discipleship Training

Unless otherwise noted, Scripture quotations are from the Holy Bible, New International Version,
Copyright © 1973, 1978, 1984 by International Bible Society. Used by permission.

Other versions used:

Revised Standard Version of the Bible (RSV), copyrighted, 1946, 1952,
© 1971, 1973. Used by permission.

King James Version (KJV)

New King James Version (NKJV). Copyright © 1979, 1980, 1982,
Thomas Nelson, Inc., Publishers. Used by permission.

THE MESSAGE. Copyright © by Eugene H. Peterson, 1993, 1994, 1995.
Used by permission of NavPress Publishing Group.

Cover Design: Edward Crawford

Printed in the United States of America

LifeWay Press
127 Ninth Avenue North
Nashville, TN 37234-0150

Additional copies of the general edition of this resource (Item # 0-7673-9850-5) can be ordered by writing or
calling the Customer Service Center at 1-800-458-2772; 127 Ninth Avenue North, Nashville, TN 37234-
0113. They are also available by visiting the nearest LifeWay Christian Store or order online at
www.lifeway.com.

Letter to Church Leaders

Spiritual transformation is God's work of changing a believer into the likeness of Jesus by creating a new identity in Christ and by empowering a lifelong relationship of love, trust, and obedience to glorify God.

Transformational discipleship is what happens in a church when its members have experienced spiritual transformation. Every program, every ministry in the life of a church should have the goal to help believers be transformed into the likeness of Jesus.

When believers come to know Jesus personally, the character of Jesus spills over into the activities of the church so that character-based, internal, spiritual transformation becomes the goal rather than activity-based performance. Church members today have extensive head knowledge about God but don't really *know* God well enough to believe Him when He gives a directive in life. Many of our churches are being merely remodeled by activities and programs driven by man, rather than being transformed by God.

Are you and your church ready to truly *know* God, to transition from head knowledge of God to heart-to-heart intimacy with Him? Through the relationship of love, trust, and obedience that Jesus modeled, God will carry you and your church to the proper destination. The rewards that come from spiritual transformation are nothing short of miraculous. Your church focused on transformational discipleship is a church focused on Jesus. As a believer, as a leader, can you think of a better focal point?

At the end of each chapter are some questions and activities. Please don't just quickly read over these, but prayerfully and intentionally examine your ministry and the ministry of your church as you read and answer the questions and complete the activities. There is no boundary to what you and your ministry can become as you yield your life to constantly abiding in Jesus. We will be praying for you as you begin this journey of transformation.

Barry Sneed

Roy T. Edgemon

Table of Contents

NOTE:
You may want to purchase a spiral notebook to use along with this workbook. This workbook contains rules in the margin and a few note pages at the end of this book for your use, but as you examine your ministry and the ministry of your church, you will need more space for your responses and planning. Throughout each chapter, and at the end of each chapter, are questions and activities that require additional paper. As you embark on this journey of spiritual transformation, consider using a file folder to store your workbook, spiral notebook, testimonies, and other information that you request and receive from those in your church. Your file folder will be a handy reference for you as your church begins a transformational discipleship ministry.

IMPORTANT QUESTION

The question you must first ask is this: What does God want us to do with our lives as believers?

The answer is this…

> Therefore, I urge you, brothers, in view of God's mercy to offer your bodies as living sacrifices holy and pleasing to God—this is your spiritual act of worship. Do not conform any longer to the pattern of this world, but be transformed by the renewing of your mind. Then you will be able to test and approve what God's will is—his good, pleasing and perfect will (Rom. 12:1-2).

That means—make no excuses—the old way has to go…

> You were taught, with regard to your former way of life to put off your old self, which is being corrupted by its deceitful desires; to be made new in the attitude of your minds; and to put on the new self, created to be like God in true righteousness and holiness (Eph. 4:22-24).

So what does that mean for believers today? If we were to answer this question with one word, it would be to *abide*. Spiritual transformation is so beautifully demonstrated in the words of Jesus in John 15 (RSV). Jesus uses the word *abide* 10 times in 10 verses. To understand the word *abide*, we must understand the illustration that Jesus gives about the vineyard.

Jesus says He is the true Vine. The word *true* refers to the "genuine" or the "real" Vine. In the Old Testament Israel is pictured as the vineyard that is a disappointment to God. Hosea described Israel as a luxuriant vine but without fruit (Hos. 10:1). Isaiah described God's investment in Israel as a farmer who invested in a vineyard; but when the fruit was produced, it was wild and bitter grapes (Isa. 5:1-7). In Jeremiah, God said to the nation of Israel, *Yet I had planted thee a noble vine, wholly a right seed: how then art thou turned into the degenerate plant of a strange vine unto me?* (Jer. 2:21, KJV).

Israel was so taken with this image of being God's vineyard that the sculpture over the temple gate was that of a golden vine. In John 15, Jesus is declaring to the world that He is God's real Vine. Using the language of the vine-grower, Jesus describes a living union between His disciples and Himself. Just as He is connected to the Father, Jesus' disciples must be connected to Him in a living fellowship. Jesus says that there are branches that bear fruit and others that bear none. Disciples who make a public profession of faith, but have no practice or who talk with no deeds are branches without fruit.

Jesus describes God as the vine keeper. It is the relationship of Jesus to the Father that calls for the relationship between Jesus and His disciples. It is the Divine Vine Keeper who cares for the vine, tends it, and watches for the fruit. The Divine Vine Keeper plants it, prunes it, and will receive glory from it.

Jesus teaches us to live in His personal Spirit, which He once described as *"the Son can do nothing by himself"* (John 5:19). Jesus lived dependent upon the Father. *"As for the person who hears my words but does not keep them, I do not judge him. For I did not come to judge the world, but to save it. There is a judge for the one who rejects me and does not accept my words; that very word which I spoke will condemn him at the last day. For I did not speak of my own accord, but the Father who sent me commanded me what to say and how to say it. I know that his command leads to eternal life. So whatever I say is just what the Father has told me to say"* (John 12:47-50). Jesus made it clear that His words carried the ultimate weight of the Father. Jesus spoke and lived with perfect authority, because God Himself was directing every word He spoke and every action He took.

God watched over Jesus so as to develop, by His personal direction, the true fruit by which humanity would glorify God through their lives and actions. He sought nothing less than to spiritually transform humankind to become like Jesus. God's nature living in humanity, possesses the virtues of individual character that are adequate to all needs of all times and all ages.

When God as the Vine Keeper finds branches that are filled with their own independent will and contradictory purposes that impair their natural purpose, it is His task to clip, water, prune, and love those branches until they fulfill His purpose in bringing glory to God. The Father cares for the branch as having the life of heaven. As it is the extension of His own Son, God cares for the branch with all the love which He has for His only begotten Son. The love between the Father and the Son flows into the branches.

Jesus teaches us to pray, *Our Father which art in heaven* (Matt. 6:9, KJV). Jesus said in His great, priestly, prayer in John 17:20-21, *Neither pray I for these alone, but for them also which shall believe on me through their word; that they all may be one; as thou, Father, art in me, and I in thee, that they also may be one in us: that the world may believe that thou hast sent me* (KJV). After His resurrection Jesus said to Mary, *Touch me not; for I am not yet ascended to my Father: but go to my brethren, and say unto them, I ascend unto my Father, and your Father; and to my God, and your God* (John 20:17, KJV). The hand that touches the vine to prune and cultivate is the hand that moves with the purpose of the Father's heart.

The sole glory of the vine then is fruitfulness; so God makes fruitfulness the test. Not the leaf, the color, the strength, or the width—but the fruit is the glory of the vine. God's test is not profession, not privilege, not apparent power but the fruit of the spirit in life and power. Fruit is the evidence that Jesus abides in the soul. Jesus said, *Ye shall know them by their fruits* (Matt. 7:16, KJV). The branch that is in Christ has all that is necessary to become fruitful; and, if it is unfruitful, the supernatural power is dormant and the branch is left with a deadness that will be cut off.

Pruning the Vine

Jesus said that His Father will purge or cleanse the branches that do bear fruit. A vine that is well-tended grows so fast that it must be pruned to conserve its energy to bear fruit and not just grow and produce nonfruit-bearing branches. If the branch were allowed to grow unchecked, many of the blossoms would never fruit. They would form tendrils instead of clusters; the vine keeper cuts the excess branch to allow the sap to fill the clusters and produce fruit. All summer long the knife is used to keep the fruit growing and to prevent wasted energy.

God uses His words as the knife to cleanse and purge believer's lives. Studying the teachings of Jesus guides us to know what should be cut from our lives. Convictions come quickly to believers at the moment they are saved. God cuts out much of our former language and this prunes us for godly speech. God convicts us of our dishonesties and thievery. He continues through His Word to purge our lives to become more and more like Jesus. All true Christians are purified by God so that we can be more useful. He takes away that which hinders our usefulness. He makes us more pure in motive and in life. God takes away the popular idols in our lives. He removes objects that bind our affections and render us inactive. As he takes away our crutches, we become more dependent on Him, and live more to the honor of God and bring forth more fruit out of humble obedience and true fidelity. God makes us clean—not perfect—but we are under the process of being purified by His teachings.

Abiding Faith

After we understand that the Father is our Vine Keeper and how He is related to Jesus, we are now able to understand what it means to abide in Jesus who says, *Abide in me, and I in you. As the branch cannot bear fruit of itself, except it abide in the vine; no more can ye, except ye abide in me* (John 15:4, KJV). The branch has no other responsibility except to receive from the vine through the roots and sap all of its nourishment. If we would recognize that through the Holy Spirit, then, our relationship to Jesus would be the most important thing in our lives. We would not grow weary in God's work if we only concentrated on our relationship to Jesus.

We believe *abide* was one of Jesus' favorite words. Jesus used several forms of the Greek word, *meno*. It means "to stay, stand fast, stay where you are, not stir, or to remain as before." As used in John 15, it means to dwell always with Jesus, to be continually operative in Jesus, in His influence and energy; to be rooted and knit to Him by the Holy Spirit. Thayer quotes Ruckert, "something has established itself permanently within my soul, and always exerts its power in me."[1] Abide has the idea of permanence of position, holding and maintaining unbroken communion and fellowship with Jesus. The Christian is to exercise absolute, unalterable dependence upon Jesus. Jesus said that this is the way fruit comes into our life, and without this continuous connection there is no fruit. *For without me ye can do nothing* (John 15:5, KJV). Andrew Murray says, "If I am something, then God is not everything; but when I become nothing, God can become all, and the everlasting God in Christ can reveal Himself fully."[2] Abiding is the continuous act by which the Christian lays aside all he might draw from his own wisdom, strength, and good, to desire all from Christ alone.

The secret to the life of Jesus was His constant contact with the Father. Mark writes, *Very early in the morning, while it was still dark, Jesus got up, left the house and went off to a solitary place, where he prayed* (Mark 1:35). *He went up into a mountain apart to pray: and when the evening was come, he was there alone* (Matt. 14:23, KJV) *He departed again into a mountain himself alone* (John 6:15, KJV). These verses illustrate Jesus was abiding in God. We must follow the example of Jesus. Without that constant contact with God, we can do nothing.

Jesus promised in John 14:16-17, *And I will pray to the Father, and he shall give you another Comforter, that he may abide with you forever; even the Spirit of truth; whom the world cannot receive, because it seeth him not, neither knoweth him: but ye know him; for he dwelleth with you, and shall be in you* (KJV). God has made a wonderful provision for us to abide in Him. We have the Holy Spirit living in us and His Word, the Bible, to guide us to all truth. It is essential that we have both the Word of Truth and the continuous contact with the Spirit of Truth—the Holy Spirit. There is always the danger of dead orthodoxy without the power of Holiness living in us. A dead branch on a tree was not always dead. It was produced by the life force of the tree. It died when the sap of the tree was no longer flowing through its branch.

Fruitful Disciples

God's purpose in abiding in us is that we produce fruit. Notice how often Jesus uses the word *fruit* in John 15 (KJV). *Every branch in me that beareth not fruit he taketh away: and every branch that beareth fruit, he purgeth it, that it may bring forth more fruit* (v. 2). *As the branch cannot bear fruit of itself, except it abide in the vine; no more can ye, except you abide in me* (v. 4). *He that abideth in me, and I in him, the same bringeth forth much fruit* (v. 5). *Herein is my Father glorified, that ye bear much fruit; so shall ye be my disciples* (v. 8). *Ye have not chosen me, but I have chosen you, and ordained you, that ye should go and bring forth fruit, and that your fruit should remain: that whatsoever ye shall ask of the Father in my name, he may give it to you* (v. 16).

What is the fruit that Jesus wants the Christian to produce? Listen to Jesus in Luke 19:10, *"For the Son of Man came to seek and to save what was lost."* Jesus said this after He had called Zacchaeus down from the tree and went to his house to spend the night. Zacchaeus repented of his sins and made restitution, and Jesus said, *"Today salvation has come to this house, because this man, too, is a son of Abraham"* (Luke 19:9).

Jesus built His church on Peter's confession that Jesus is the Christ (Matt. 16:13-20). The believer is to take the message of the gospel to the whole world before Christ comes again. *"This gospel of the kingdom will be preached in the whole world as a testimony to all nations, then the end will come"* (Matt. 24:14). The fruit, which Jesus expects from Christians, is the conversion of people to the gospel. It is the ingathering of souls into the kingdom of God. The demand for fruit is an expression of God's love to humanity in the revelation of the Savior's loving compassion for those who are lost in sin and darkness. The fruit God expects is the result of every believer telling his world of God's love and salvation.

If we are abiding in Christ, sharing our faith with others is as natural as breathing. We are telling the story of the One whom we love more than anything else in our lives. Our lives will be full of stories of His constant action in and around our daily living.

The second fruit of the Christian is to see the world drawn to the love of God when they can see Jesus in the lives of Christians. In Matthew 7:15, Jesus taught how to recognize false teachers and prophets by their fruit. *"Watch out for false prophets. They come to you in sheep's clothing but inwardly they are ferocious wolves. By their fruit you will recognize them. Do people pick grapes from thorn bushes, or figs from thistles? Likewise every good tree bears good fruit, but a bad tree bears bad fruit. A good tree cannot bear bad fruit, and a bad tree cannot bear good fruit. Every tree that does not bear good fruit is cut down and thrown into the fire. Thus, by their fruit you will recognize them."* Jesus uses the same illustration in Matthew 12:33. Luke enlarges the parable in Luke 6:45: *"The good man brings good things out of the good stored up in his heart, and the evil man brings evil things out of the evil stored up in his heart. For out of the overflow of his heart his mouth speaks."* The apostle Paul pulls these teachings together in Galatians 5:22-23: *But the fruit of the Spirit is love, joy, peace, patience, kindness, goodness, faithfulness, gentleness and self-control. Against such things there is no law.* These nine graces of Christian character together form the fruit of the Spirit, one and indivisible. When the Holy Spirit is free to work in our lives He does not produce one grace without the other. This is called Christlikeness or holiness. God's fruit in us is general in it's character, supernatural in its origin, gradual in its growth, and natural in its development. Paul wrote in Philippians 1:11 that Christians are to be *filled with the fruit of righteousness that comes through Jesus Christ—to the glory and praise of God.*

Paul prayed for the Colossians in Colossians 1:9-10, *Asking God to fill you with the knowledge of his will through all spiritual wisdom and understanding. And we pray this in order that you may live a life worthy of the Lord and may please him in every way: bearing fruit in every good work, growing in the knowledge of God.* Evangelism and character are then the fruits of the spirit. John Bunyan wrote, "If I were fruitless it mattered not who commended me; if I were fruitful, I cared not who did condemn."[3]

When the individual bears the fruit of Jesus, the Father is glorified.

When the Christian is abounding in good works the Lord is honored, the church is strengthened, and the individual is blessed. Fruits show the power of the gospel over evil and the power to restore the Christian to the divine image of Jesus. Paul described the fruitful life in Philippians 4:7: *And the peace of God, which transcends all understanding will guard your hearts and your minds in Christ Jesus. Finally, brothers, whatever is true, whatever is noble, whatever is right, whatever is pure, whatever is lovely, whatever is admirable—if anything is excellent or praiseworthy—think about such things.* Thinking on these high and lofty planes bring honor to the God who lifted us out of the filthy-mind gutters of the world. When our lives reflect Jesus, God is honored. Our mind—like our heart—is now filled with Jesus—we are being spiritually transformed into His likeness.

The Results of Abiding

Abiding in Jesus gives us confidence in prayer. Twice in John 15:7,16, Jesus says if we abide in Him we have power in prayer. Jesus teaches us that our waking hours should be a continuous experience of communion with Him. To do this means that we will arrange our lives, prayers, and silence in a way that Jesus is consciously present throughout the day. Henry Ward Beecher said, "Let the day have a blessed baptism by giving your first waking thoughts to God. The first hour of the morning is the rudder of the day."[4] G. Campbell Morgan translates verse 7, "If you abide in Me, and My words abide in you, you shall demand as you're due whatever you are inclined to, and it shall be generated unto you."[5] These are the strongest words in the Bible in regard to prayer. If we abide in Jesus and His Word, we will never ask anything that is out of harmony with His will. In this state of abiding, God is willing to call in generated power or creative power to meet our requests. Miracles come from this kind of praying. In verses 9-17, Jesus tells us that we have been chosen by Him and ordained by Him to bring forth fruit and that the fruit we bring forth is eternal (v. 16). Notice the four calls that Jesus gives in this passage.

• **Jesus calls us to love.** Just as Jesus came to us with the call of God's love, we are to take that call to the world. We are to love one another as the Father loves the Son and the Son loves us. We are to continue in this love and never let it grow cold. Jesus writes to the church in Ephesus in Revelation 2:4, *Nevertheless I have somewhat against thee, because thou hast left thy first love* (KJV). We are to keep the love for

God on the front burner of our heart and never allow the fire to go out. Paul exhorted young Timothy to *fan into flame the gift of God, which is in you* (2 Tim. 1:6). We demonstrate our love for Jesus, as we love one another. Listen to what Jesus said about our love that last night before He was killed on the cross. *"A new commandment I give unto you, that ye love one another; as I have loved you, that ye also love one another. By this shall all men know that ye are my disciples, if ye have love one to another"* (John 13:34-35). *If ye love me keep my commandments* (John 14:15, KJV). *"He that hath my commandments, and keepth them,…I will love him, and will manifest myself to him"* (John 14:21). *If a man love me, he will keep my words: and my Father will love him, and we will come unto him, and make our abode with him. He that loveth me not keepeth not my sayings: and the word which ye hear is not mine, but the Father's which sent me* (John 14:23-24, KJV). *But that the world may know that I love the Father; and as the Father gave me commandment, even so I do* (John 14:31,KJV). *As the Father hath loved me, so have I loved you: continue ye in my love. If ye keep my commandments, ye shall abide in my love; even as I have kept my Father's commandments, and abide in his love* (John 15:9-10, KJV). *This is my commandment, That ye love one another, as I have loved you. Greater love hath no man than this, that a man lay down his life for his friends. Ye are my friends, if ye do whatsoever I command you* (John 15:12-14, KJV). *"These things I command you, that ye love one another"* (John 15:17).

We demonstrate our love to God by living in His words and obeying them and by loving one another. The beloved disciple John says, *And so we know and rely on the love God has for us. God is love. Whoever lives in love lives in God, and God in him. In this way, love is made complete among us so that we will have confidence on the day of judgment, because in this world we are like him. There is no fear in love. But perfect love drives out fear, because fear has to do with punishment. The one who fears is not made perfect in love. We love because he first loved us. If anyone says, "I love God," yet hates his brother, he is a liar. For anyone who does not love his brother, whom he has seen, cannot love God, whom he has not seen. And he has given us this command: Whoever loves God must also love his brother* (1 John 4:16-21).

• **Jesus calls us to joy.** Jesus said, *These things have I spoken unto you, that my joy might remain in you, and that your joy might be full* (John 15:11, KJV). This is the first time in His ministry that He refers to His joy. Yet this is the night when He will experience unfathomable sorrow.

Listen to what He will say in the garden in just a little while. *"My soul is overwhelmed with sorrow to the point of death"* (Matt. 26:38). *And being in anguish, he prayed more earnestly, and his sweat was like drops of blood falling to the ground* (Luke 22:44). The writer of Hebrews says about that last night: *Let us fix our eyes on Jesus, the author and perfecter of our faith, who for the joy set before him endured the cross, scorning its shame, and sat down at the right hand of the throne of God* (Heb. 12:2).

The second time Jesus spoke of His joy was the same night in His great prayer in John 17:13, *"I am coming to you now, but I say these things while I am still in the world, so that they may have the full measure of my joy within them."* Jesus' joy was that He had fulfilled the plan of God for 33 years. He had lived without sin and was now ready to be lifted up as the perfect sin offering to God for the sins of all humanity. "Joy is the fruit of a right relationship with God. It is not something people can create by their own efforts."[6] Jesus has not only the joy in His purpose that is almost completed, but in the joy of those eleven disciples who will carry His message to the world. In the second part of verse 11, He refers to the disciple's joy as full, fulfilled, or complete. When we begin our journey with Jesus there will be wonderful and passionate outbreaks of joy, but this language implies that the joy will be more stable and consistent as we grow to spiritual maturity. The statement—the longer we serve and love Jesus, the sweeter He grows—is true.

A.B. Bruce says, "Joy in the highest sense is one of the ripe fruits of the Holy Spirit, the reward of perseverance and fidelity."[7] If we do not grow and are unfruitful in our lives, we will not have joy but sorrows and unhappiness. We will not hear the Master say, *Enter thou into the joy of thy lord* (Matt. 25:23, KJV).

• **Jesus calls us to friendship.** *Greater love hath no man than this, that a man lay down his life for his friends. Ye are my friends, if ye do whatsoever I command you. Henceforth I call you not servants; for the servant knoweth not what his lord doeth: but I have called you friends; for all things that I have heard of my Father I have made known unto you* (John 15:13-15, KJV). Up to this time Jesus had called His disciples servants or *douloi*. This is a title of honor. Moses was called the *doulos* of God or the servant of God in Deuteronomy 34:5. Joshua was called the *doulos* of God in Joshua 24:29. David was God's *doulos* in Psalm 89:20. Paul used the title *doulos* in Titus 1:1. This title is used to describe God's honor roll of His best. In the Old Testament Abraham was the friend of God (see Isa. 41:8, 2 Chron. 20:7).

Jesus is called the friend of sinners in Matthew 11:19. He calls the disciples friends in our study passage John 15:13-15 and in Luke 12:4 *"I tell you my friends, do not be afraid of those who kill the body and after that can do no more."* What a privilege to be friends of Jesus! We are His friends because we keep His teachings. He has told us all that we need to know about the kingdom of God. We are His partners and He has shared His heart and His mind with us. We know His plans and His purpose in the world. We work with Him as joint heirs to heaven.

Paul says it well in Romans 8:15-17, *For you did not receive a spirit that makes you a slave again to fear, but you received the Spirit of sonship. And by him we cry "Abba, Father." The Spirit himself testifies with our spirit that we are God's children…then we are heirs—heirs of God and co-heirs with Christ, if indeed we share in his sufferings in order that we may also share in his glory.* If you abide in Jesus you have a special and growing friendship with the King of Kings.

• **Jesus has ordained us for His service.** *Ye have not chosen me, but I have chosen you, and ordained you, that ye should go and bring forth fruit, and that your fruit should remain: that whatsoever ye shall ask of the Father in my name, he may give it you* (John 15:16, KJV). Jesus did not write a book and lay out all of His instructions on how to build the kingdom of God. As far as we know Jesus never wrote even a letter. Instead He carefully picked out a group of people chosen one at a time and wrote into their hearts His plan for the kingdom of God. They became living books on which He had imprinted His love and message. Jesus wanted the world to see, touch, and feel His message—not just read it. Later, His disciples, under the power of the Holy Spirit, told His message in print, but Jesus has always allowed people to be His living message. Jesus has always wanted us to know Him by heart.

God designed His method of salvation. He alone initiated salvation and invites people to follow Him. The word *choose* is the Greek word *exelexathe* which means "to select out of possible options that are free from any determining forces or circumstances." The word literally means "to choose something for oneself." Those chosen have the opportunity to accept their availability of service. This doctrine is called election, which is God's plan to bring salvation to His people and His world. The Bible uses words like *choose, predestinate, save, ordain,* and *call* to indicate that God has entered into a special relationship with individuals and groups through whom He has decided to fulfill His purpose within the history of salvation. God's providence allows Him to guide human history to accomplish His purposes even when allowing human freedom and human sin. Election affirms that God is personally involved in our history. God's personal presence accomplishes His saving will. It is the creator God who calls you to abide in Him and has chosen you to go into His world and bring forth fruit. As God's elected people, we represent Christ's physical presence in the world, endeavoring to carry out God's ministry of calling a lost world to Himself.

Christ has chosen us as His disciples to bear fruit for Him by living obedient lives and leading others to know Him. This kind of fruit remains for all eternity. As we bear this kind of fruit we must never forget how important it is to love one another. As the apostle John reminds us again: *God is love. Whoever lives in love lives in God, and God in him* (1 John 4:16). What does God want us to do with our lives? Abide in Jesus, as Jesus abides in the Father. As we abide in Him, we are spiritually transformed into His likeness.

GET PERSONAL ⇨ *How this applies to you and your church…*
Since you can never lead anyone beyond where you are yourself, you must let nothing interfere with your own abiding relationship with Jesus. Describe how you are connected to Jesus in a living fellowship. Are you producing fruit? Is your ministry producing fruit?

List the times in your life when you have been pruned by God. Were you more useful and obedient to God after the pruning?

What can you do as a church leader to demonstrate more clearly to others that you have an abiding relationship with Jesus?

GET GOING ⇨ *Tips for proactive discipleship…*
1. Using our description of "abiding in Christ" (p. 8) as a guide, develop a key-word Bible study on the word *abide*. Use this study to help those you lead better understand the central importance of a Christ-centered life and its crucial role in spiritual transformation.

2. Read back through the Scriptures mentioned in this chapter everyday for 2–3 weeks. Meditate and study *abiding, the vine, the branch, the fruit*. Ask others to study these passages and share their insights.

3. Ask people to identify how church would be different if the relation-

ship to Jesus was the most important aspect of church life and the people in the community.

4. Ask a farmer to share insights about these terms in a worship service.

5. Look for testimonies that can be shared on transformed lives from people who are growing in their walk and who are bearing fruit in love, joy, friendship, and service.

6. Regularly challenge people to realize the actions they take everyday should have a foundation in the relationship they have with Christ.

7. Ask people to pray and fast and to meditate on these ideas. Seek to lead people to know God's will for your church.

8. Challenge every leader in various ministries to focus on building and growing their relationship continually and ask them to share.

9. Look for testimonies that can be shared on transformed lives from people who are growing in their walk and who are bearing fruit in love, joy, friendship, and service.

10. Speak to those who have failed or who have been cut off from the vine and how He seeks to restore them.

11. Regularly challenge people to realize the actions they take everyday should have a foundation in their abiding relationship with Christ.

[1] Kenneth S. Wuest, *Wuest's Word Studies From the Greek New Testament, Vol. 3* (Grand Rapids, Michigan: Wm. B. Eerdmans Pub. Co., 1973) 65.
[2] Andrew Murray, *Absolute Surrender* (Chicago: Moody Press) 115.
[3] John Bunyan, *Grace Abounding: A Brief Account* (www.acacia.pair.com/acacia.John Bunyan/sermons.allegories/grace.abounding/account.ministry.html).
[4] Henry Ward Beecher, *A Dictionary of Thoughts*, Tryon Edwards, D.D. (Detroit: F.B. Dickerson Co., 1915), 363.
[5] G. Campbell Morgan, D.D. *The Gospel According to John* (Westwood, New Jersey: Fleming Revell Co.) 254.
[6] Trent Butler, Ed., *Holman Bible Dictionary*, (Nashville: Holman Bible Publishers, 1991) 819.
[7] A. B. Bruce, D.D. *The Training of the Twelve* (Kregel Pub., 1971) 421.

A MAN WHO "GOT IT"

You're a church leader. Church leadership carries immense responsibility and influence. Think about when you die, how do you *want* to be remembered? Now, here's the tougher question: How will you *actually* be remembered? It's a sobering question.

Will it be said of you, "She was a nice person..." Or perhaps, "She worked hard for her family, her church, and her friends..." Or maybe, "He was a dedicated church leader who kept his focus on church growth... ." Or even, "He kept this church going during the hard times."

Granted, all these would be nice eulogies. But, once spoken, such words would be as lifeless as you resting in your coffin. They would have no lasting legacy, no real life of their own.

That wasn't the case in the life of missionary Frank Laubach. His legacy had life. What was said of him is still having a lasting impact on people today. What was said of Frank? Things like this:

"When others were with him they felt they were in the presence of Jesus. They came to know the personality of Jesus because they knew Frank." That's how Frank Laubach is remembered. How did this happen? Just as Jesus walked this earth constantly aware of the presence of God His Father, Frank lived in constant awareness of the presence of Jesus. He did this purposely, passionately, and consistently.

Before you place Frank on some grand, not-to-be-attained-by-ordinary-man pedestal, know this. Frank's intimate relationship with God did not happen overnight. Frank experienced a spiritual transformation that slowly worked its way from the inside out. This inside-out transformation had a dramatic impact on Frank as he experienced the presence of God. Frank's spiritual transformation was so evident, powerful, and life-changing that those who met him experienced God, too.

This record of Frank's experiences (from letters to his father) are recorded in a book, *Letters By a Modern Mystic*. We are able to look inside the mind, heart, and soul of this man of God and see this life-change process. In this first entry Frank mentions "a profound dissatisfaction" that drives him. Perhaps this unrest mirrors your own; we know it mirrored ours. May you, too, take to heart the same source for its cure.

January 20, 1930

Although I have been a minister and a missionary for 15 years, I have not lived the entire day of every day, minute by

> **God is waiting for you to lay your to-do-list at His feet and abide in Him.**

minute to follow the will of God. Two years ago a profound dissatisfaction led me to begin trying to line up my actions with the will of God about every 15 minutes or every half hour. Other people to whom I confessed this intention said it was impossible. I judge from what I have heard that few people are really trying even that. But this year I have started out to live all my waking moments in conscious listening to the inner voice, asking without ceasing, "What, Father, do you desire said? What, Father, do you desire this minute?" It is clear that this is exactly what Jesus was doing all day every day.

Note Frank's last sentence: "It is clear that this is exactly what Jesus was doing every day." Frank knew he was on to something vital. This conscious listening to the inner voice of God would erase the dissatisfaction in his life. You see, Frank was about to "get it."

Let's read on as Frank takes us further into his heart.

January 29, 1930

I feel simply carried along each hour, doing my part in a plan which is far beyond myself. This sense of cooperation with God in little things is what so astonishes me, for I never have felt it this way before. I need something, and turn round to find it waiting for me. I must work, to be sure, but there is God working along with me. God takes care of all the rest. My part is to live this hour in continuous conversation with God and in perfect responsiveness to his will, to make this hour gloriously rich. This seems to be all I need to think about.

After 15 years in the ministry Frank had an astounding revelation. Frank's life changed when he focused on being in tune to God's will—on being just like Jesus. He laid aside all the things he had previously thought were important and anything that was discordant with God. Frank's life became rich because his purpose for being on earth became amazingly clear: His life was to glorify God, just as the life of Jesus glorified God. Frank realized, the more he became like Jesus the more he glorified God. After years of ministry, Frank Laubach finally "got it."

Jesus glorified God by being like His Father. It was by setting His life straight out to God that Jesus showed the world God's loving and merciful heart.

The Word became flesh and made his dwelling among us. We have seen his glory, the glory of the One and Only, who came from the Father, full of grace and truth. For the law was given through Moses; grace and truth came through Jesus Christ. No one has ever seen God, but God the One and Only, who is at the Father's side, has made him known (John 1:14,17-18).

The MESSAGE states it this way in John 1:14,17-18. *"This one-of-a-kind God-expression, who exists at the very heart of the Father, has made him plain as day."*

By practicing the presence of God, by following the example of Jesus and setting his own life straight out to God, Frank, too, was drawn to the very heart of God—and he made the heart of God as plain as day to others.

March 1, 1930

The sense of being led by an unseen hand which takes mine while another hand reaches ahead and prepares the way, grows upon me daily. I do not need to strain at all to find opportunity....Perhaps a man who has been an ordained minister [for 15 years] ought to be ashamed to confess that he never before felt the joy of complete hourly, minute by minute—now what shall I call it?—more than surrender. I had that before. More than listening to God. I tried that before. I cannot find the word that will mean to you or to me what I am now experiencing. It is a "will" act. I compel my mind to open straight out toward God. I wait and listen with determined sensitiveness. I fix my attention there, and sometimes it requires a long time...After a while, perhaps, it will become a habit, and the sense of effort will grow less.

The words of Frank Laubach make it clear: God was transforming Frank and the way Frank related to Him. Frank had a God-hunger, a deep need to be not a breath away from the presence of God. But it was a new relationship, and Frank had questions.

March 23, 1930

One question now to be put to the test is this: Can we have that contact with God all the time? All the time awake, fall asleep in His arms, and awaken in His presence? Can we at-

tain that? Can we do His will all the time? Can we think His thoughts all the time?

Frank discovered that, for those attuned to the spiritually transformed life, the answer to his questions was yes. Jesus was in contact with God all the time. He awoke, walked, worked, and slept in God's presence at all times. He did God's will. He thought God's thoughts. Because Frank set his heart on being like Jesus, he experienced the same joy Jesus must have felt when He proclaimed, *"I am in the Father and the Father is in me"* (John 14:11a). It was a relationship like no other.

April 18, 1930

I have tasted a thrill in fellowship with God which has made anything discordant with God disgusting. This afternoon the possession of God has caught me up with such sheer joy that I thought I never had known anything like it. God was so close and so amazingly lovely that I felt like melting all over with a strange blissful contentment. Having had this experience, which comes to me now several times a week, the thrill of filth repels me, for I know its power to drag me from God. And after an hour of close fellowship with God my soul feels clean, as new fallen snow.

Frank was a man transformed. He was constantly compelled to be more and more like Jesus and continually repelled by anything unlike Him. He was Romans 12:1-2 on legs:

"So here's what I want you to do, God helping you: Take your everyday, ordinary life—your sleeping, eating, going-to-work, and walking-around life—and place it before God as an offering.…Don't become so well-adjusted to your culture that you fit into it without even thinking. Instead, fix your attention on God. You'll be changed from the inside out (Rom. 12:1-2, The MESSAGE).

Frank Laubach was changed from the inside out. After 15 years in the ministry, he finally "got it." He dedicated every day of the rest of his life to becoming more like Jesus. Frank was no longer satisfied with mediocre Christianity. He had taken to heart Paul's words in Ephesians 4:22-23 that Christ brings together belief and behavior.

That's no life for you. You learned Christ! My assumption is that you have paid careful attention to him, been well instructed in the truth precisely as we have it in Jesus. Since, then, we do not have the excuse of ignorance, everything—and I do mean everything—connected with that old way of life has to go. It's rotten through and through. Get rid of it! And then take on an entirely new way of life—a God-fashioned life, a life renewed from the inside and working itself into your conduct as God accurately reproduces his character in you (Eph. 4:22-23, The MESSAGE).

No, mediocre Christianity was not enough for Frank Laubach. A Sunday-morning, Wednesday-night relationship with God was not enough for this man. He thirsted for the same constant companionship with God that Jesus had while He was on earth.

May 14, 1930

Oh, this thing of keeping in constant touch with God, of making Him the object of my thought and the companion of my conversations, is the most amazing thing I ever ran across. It is working. I cannot do it even half of a day—not yet, but I believe I shall be doing it some day for the entire day. It is a matter of acquiring a new habit of thought. Now I like the Lord's presence so much that when for a half hour or so He slips out of mind—as He does many times a day—I feel as though I had deserted Him, and as though I had lost something very precious in my life.

Frank Laubach wanted to be like Jesus so that God would be glorified. It was as simple as that. Because Frank's desire was so pure and God's power to transform so great, an amazing thing happened—Frank did become like Jesus. God created in him that same "marvelous pull" that Jesus had when He walked the roads of earth each day—that same pull that draws people to Jesus today. Although Frank Laubach died years ago, his life continues to draw people to Jesus because Frank became so much like his Savior. That, friends, is a lasting legacy.

June 1, 1930

Last Monday was the most completely successful day of my life to date, so far as giving my day in complete and continuous surrender to God is concerned—though I shall hope for far better days—and I remember how as I looked at people with a love God gave, they looked back and acted as though they wanted to go with me. I felt then that for a day I saw a little of that marvelous pull that Jesus had as He walked along the road day after day "God-intoxicated" and radiant with the endless communion of His soul with God.[8]

Frank Laubach found a great truth in his journey. He learned that he had an unlimited capacity to grow spiritually in his relationship with God. He learned that, through the power of the Holy Spirit, he could be like Jesus, honor God with his life, and by doing so marvelously point others toward God.

And that's just what Frank did, and continues to do. Frank Laubach is remembered as a man who lived as Jesus lived, a man who loved as Jesus loved, a man who trusted as Jesus trusted, and a man who obeyed God just as Jesus obeyed Him.

As a church leader, isn't that how you really want to be remembered? Isn't that what churches are for—to help people honor and glorify God with their lives? As a leader in your church don't you want to be the kind of person God can use to lead people to be spiritually transformed—to love, trust, and obey Him, to be like Jesus.

This resource has been written to help you focus yourself and your church on a vital and common purpose: to become like Jesus and help others become like Him. Becoming like Jesus is the essence of spiritual transformation. That is what Frank Laubach experienced. Jesus wants you and every believer in your church to experience spiritual transformation—to be spiritually transformed to be like Him.

After you complete this book, we strongly encourage you to complete the study *Jesus By Heart*, which presents the heartbeat of spiritual transformation in a personal way. The following chapter is a summary of the key elements of spiritual transformation discussed in detail in *Jesus By Heart*.

We commend you as you take this next step in your journey to become like Jesus and seek to help lead a transformational discipleship ministry that helps others in your church become like Him, too. Ironically, what you will discover is that guiding others to become like Jesus has been God's supreme purpose for the church all along.

GET THIS ⇨ *The heart of this chapter…*

You (and every believer in your church) have an unlimited capacity to grow spiritually in your relationship with God. Through the power of the Holy Spirit, you can be like Jesus, to love, trust, and obey God with your life, and by doing so God will marvelously pull others toward Himself through you.

GET PERSONAL ⇨ *How this applies to you and your church…*

What things in your life will change if you take your *everyday, ordinary life—your sleeping, eating, going to work, and walking around life—and place it before God as an offering?* (*The MESSAGE*)

What would be the result if every believer in your church sought to love, trust, and obey God daily?

Look at and reflect on your church's weekly calendar. How would a focus on Jesus have changed your last week or month? What would you stop doing in the ministries and the programs of your church?

What steps can you take during the next month to refocus your life on becoming like Jesus and seeking to live in constant awareness of God's presence?

In the margin list two ways you can begin to immediately model the refocus of your life to your church leaders and members.

List two ways you can model your spiritual transformation to the lost in your community.

How can you change your schedule to reflect your central value of becoming more like Jesus? How do you think such a scheduling change would affect your church?

GET GOING ⇨ *Tips for proactive discipleship…*

1. Identify three or four people in your church or community that you think might model or be open to modeling a life that seeks to focus on Jesus every moment. Interview them and share Frank's story. Invite their observations and questions. Ask them to join you in seeking to journal your thoughts and prayers while seeking to daily glorify God.

2. Talk with several people who have been members of your church for a long time. Ask them to share about people or periods of time when God seemed the most real in their church. Ask them what it would take for God to do a new work in the lives of the community.

3. Consider launching a sermon series on Scriptures about spiritual transformation (see Scriptures throughout this book), or begin group studies of *Jesus By Heart* and *Jesus On Leadership*.

4. Enlist a special team of prayer warriors to petition God for a church-wide burden for spiritual transformation. Encourage them to pray specifically for leaders who share the burden to come forward or at least begin seeking to daily build a relationship with God.

5. List three proactive things you can do during the next three months to communicate to your church body that each believer has an unlimited capacity to grow in his or her relationship with God.

6. Write steps you can take in the next six months to lay the groundwork for the development of small groups to facilitate spiritual transformation in your church body.

[8]Frank Laubach, *Letters By a Modern Mystic*, 1979, xiii-xiv. New Readers Press, U. S. Publishing Division of Laubach Literacy. Used by permission.

THE HEART OF
SPIRITUAL TRANSFORMATION

As a leader in your church, the most important thing to grasp about spiritual transformation is its source. Spiritual transformation is a God-thing.

At its nucleus, spiritual transformation requires repentance and total trust in God to dramatically *change what we could never change ourselves.* Being in every worship service or taking every church class offered won't make it happen. Participating in a multitude of ministries won't bring it about. Fasting won't cinch it.

Realizing that spiritual transformation isn't something you can do is a hard pill for us to swallow as egotistical humans—and perhaps even more so as church leaders. We hate to admit we can't do something. It's easy for us to try to take spiritual transformation into our own hands—without even realizing that's what we're doing. We're compelled by the Christian and secular culture and propelled by personality quirks to get busy doing the things we perceive Christians are supposed to be doing. We have places to go, spiritual activities to do, people to see. But there exists a discouraging disparity between our efforts and the results: and, to top it off, we're exhausted. We're working at ministry. We wonder, *What's wrong? Shouldn't we be energized by serving God?*

The truth is, as church leaders, we are too often caught up in the momentum of ministry that we've forsaken our own needed moments of intimacy with God. We need to stop what we're doing, listen to our hearts, and honestly assess our own spiritual status before we can effectively lead other believers to a face-to-face relationship with God.

Take this simple test. List the spiritually-based activities you are currently involved in as a church leader and the amount of time you commit to each one in an average week. Next, list the amount of time you spend in an average week in solitude with God developing your own personal relationship with Him. Are you out of balance?

Granted, many of the activities you listed as a church leader are, most likely, worthwhile ministries. It may be that the scales are tipped the wrong way. There must be priority time set aside to nurture a personal relationship with Jesus. There must be a hunger to be in touch with God every minute of every day just as Jesus was. Just like Frank Laubach, you have an unlimited capacity to grow spiritually in your relationship with God. Through the power of the Holy Spirit, you, too,

> God is waiting for His people to lay their to-do-lists at His feet, seek His face, and abide in Him.

can be like Jesus, honor God with your life, and by doing so marvelously God will pull others toward Himself through you.

So where is your relationship with God at this moment? Here's a good measuring rod for discerning your spiritual health: *Is your personal relationship with Jesus closer today than it was this time last month? Do you sense such a growing relationship in the other leaders of your church? What about in the members of your congregation?* If the answer is repeatedly no, then it's time for a dramatic life-change—and God is the only source for this change because spiritual transformation is strictly a God-empowered miracle. It does not—and cannot—emerge from human effort. God is waiting for your repentant, obedient heart so He can miraculously, with love and grace, transform your life.

God has been waiting for the church to lay its to-do-lists at His feet, seek His face, and abide in Him. He has been waiting for His people to crave a relationship with Him. He has been waiting for His church to call His name. His has been waiting for His church to become like His Son and love, trust, and obey Him. Why? Because the heart of God is that believers be transformed into the likeness of Jesus.

Just Like Jesus
The Scriptures are ripe with lessons about becoming like Jesus. In His last conversation with His disciples before His crucifixion, Jesus made some amazing commitments to His disciples and to the church concerning spiritual transformation. He promised:
- we can love one another as He loves us (John 13:34);
- we can trust Him completely (John 14:1);
- we are in Him and He is in us (John 14:20);
- we can do what He has done—and more (John 14:12).

Those kind of amazing promises demand a miraculous change of heart no human can do alone. It requires internal metamorphosis. John the Baptist, one who never minced words, said in Luke 3:8a,9a: *"You brood of vipers!...Produce fruit in keeping with repentance....The ax is already at the root of the trees, and every tree that does not produce good fruit will be cut down and thrown into the fire."*

In no uncertain terms, John gives the proverbial boot to the activity-based-to-do-list-Christianity that is so pervasive in the church today. John stressed that believers must have a spiritual heart transplant—a selfish heart replaced by the heart of Jesus. To understand how this metamorphosis takes place, let's look at four critical questions about spiritual transformation—

1. What is spiritual transformation?
2. How does God spiritually transform a believer?
3. What are the evidences of a spiritually transformed believer?
4. What are the hindrances to spiritual transformation?

What Is Spiritual Transformation?

Spiritual transformation is God's work of changing a believer into the likeness of Jesus by creating a new identity in Christ and by empowering a lifelong relationship of love, trust, and obedience to glorify God.

Now, let's break this definition down into bite-sized pieces.

• *Spiritual transformation begins with a new identity in Christ.*

Salvation is a defining experience in which we literally become new persons. We take on the identity of Jesus. This is such a profound, definitive experience that it can be said God gives believers a new spiritual DNA, a new genetic origin, a new nature. Believers are set apart for God's glory at the moment of new birth in Christ (John 3:5-6) and they become part of the household of God—joint heirs with Christ (Eph. 2:19-20). Jesus describes the genetic link of this new identity in John 14:20: *"I am in my Father, and you are in me, and I am in you."*

What is the impact of this spiritual inheritance? Just as God gives a newborn baby the DNA code needed to grow to adulthood, He immediately gives new believers everything needed to live lives that glorify Him. God gives them everything needed to walk with Him in love, trust, and obedience—just as Jesus did. God is our Source for transformation. Spiritual growth, then, isn't about us; it's about what God wants to do in us because we are His children. Our identity as children of God is the fertile ground God uses for spiritual transformation. (See 1 Pet. 1:3b-4.) *If anyone is in Christ, he is a new creation; the old has gone, the new has come!* (2 Cor. 5:17.) To better grasp a new identity in Christ, study *My Identity in Christ* by Gene Wilkes (available June 2000).

• *Spiritual transformation continues in a growing relationship of love, trust, and obedience.*

The new identity believers have in Christ is indeed an all-surpassing miracle. But it does not mean that with this new identity believers are fully mature in Christ. While God loves the believer in an infant state of rebirth, He is not content to leave the believer in spiritual diapers. There is much growth to be encouraged. And that is where the Holy Spirit enters and begins to help develop the fullness of the new identity that the believer has received with repentance and salvation.

Spiritual transformation, then, is a progressive spiritual journey—a steady change of worldview, attitude, and behavior. It is at its foundation a change of the heart that expresses itself in the outward life. This internal character change is the result of a growing relationship of love, trust, and obedience to God.

Jesus' life represents a road map for the spiritual journeys of all believers, spiritual journeys whose first steps of love and trust lead to obedience. *"Father, if You are willing, take this cup from me; yet, not my will, but yours be done,"* Jesus said in Luke 22:42. These words were not said easily; they were wrenched from the anguished soul of Jesus as the dark shadow of the cross inched ever closer to Him.

It is clear from Scripture that Jesus had a choice in the matter. He could have walked away from the cross, but He didn't. Jesus' love and trust of the Father was so great that He chose to obey Him—no matter the cost. By choosing to obey His Father, Jesus was empowered to conduct Himself like the Father.

By choosing surrender and obedience, Jesus demonstrated God's personal character to His disciples—and to the entire world. He did so because He wanted those He loves to personally experience God—to see Him face-to-face. As a result of Jesus' love, trust, and obedience He forever changed the world.

I Surrender All—but Not Easily

Obedience. Few of us like to roll that word off our tongue. After trusting and repentance, obedience represents the crucial link to a personal relationship with God. When you and other church leaders are obedient to God the Father—just as Jesus was—you, too, have an opportunity to be more like the Father, to show your true love for Him, and to see God draw others to Himself through you. Since spiritual transformation is accomplished from the inside out, the more you surrender to becoming like Jesus, the more you will "behave" like Jesus. And the more others will be drawn to this change in you.

Don't get tripped up by the word *behave*. Spiritual transformation is not activity-based. On the contrary, it is internally charged. It is not merely doing things that mimic Christian conduct; it's an internal miracle of actually being like Jesus, taking on His identity, establishing a vital core relationship with Him in that your actions reflect an internal character change—the heart of Jesus has replaced your old, selfish heart. Jesus describes this special identity in John 14:20, *"I am in my Father, and you are in me, and I am in you."* It's Jesus living out His life through you. Everyday. In every way.

Think of it this way: My (Barry) dog, Maddie, spends almost every waking hour of her life in the presence of humans. Maddie has taken on a new identity as close as possible to human beings—eating, sleeping, taking baths, and, in almost uncanny ways, she's become "humanlike." Nevertheless, Maddie will never transform into a human; she merely conforms to the human lifestyle. Let a cat saunter into Maddie's presence and all humanlike qualities disappear.

However, you—and every believer in your church—do have a new spiritual identity, a new nature. With salvation, the Spirit of God took possession of your souls and began transforming each of you into a new creature. Unlike the external training a house dog goes through, spiritual transformation is an internal change rather than a mere transition from one way of living one's life to a different way. Jesus is actually being formed in all who belong to Him, progressively growing a deeper relationship of love, trust, and obedience (Gal. 4:19).

• *Spiritual Transformation Glorifies God.*

The goal of the new identity in Christ and a lifelong relationship of love, trust, and obedience is quite simple: to glorify God. Once again, as God intended, Jesus leads by example. Spiritual transformation requires that the believer love in the self-sacrificial way that Jesus did. *As the Father has loved me, so I have loved you. Now remain in my love* (John 15:9). *"A new command I give you: Love one another. As I have loved you, so you must love one another. By this all men will know that you are my disciples, if you love one another"* (John 13:34).

Loving God brings a responsibility to fulfill God's purposes of making His love known to the world. When a believer is truly spiritually transformed, he or she will find ways to share the love of God with others. God will be glorified when the believer is spiritually transformed.

How Does God Transform a Believer Into the Likeness of Jesus?

We've stated that true spiritual transformation must be empowered by God. When we finally yearn for a relationship with God, He begins to transform our hearts daily through the work of the Holy Spirit. Because we are here on earth, God uses real-life resources as catalysts to make us more like His Son. Let's look at some of those resources.

- *God Uses His Living Word.*

God gives His children His Word so that they will know His heart and the wisdom He has to share. His Word is the firm foundation on which believers are to establish their unique relationship with Him. The Word of God connects us with Jesus by demonstrating how Jesus lived and how He loved—and how God wants us to live. *To the Jews who had believed him, Jesus said, "If you hold to my teaching, you are really my disciples. Then you will know the truth and the truth will set you free"* (John 8:31-32). *All Scripture is God-breathed and is useful for teaching, rebuking, correcting and training in righteousness, so that the man of God may be thoroughly equipped for every good work* (2 Tim. 3:16-17).

In his book *Soul Nourishment First*, George Mueller captures the need for feeding daily on the Word. "I meditate on the Scripture, searching as it were into every verse to get a blessing out of it: not for the sake of public ministry of the Word, not for the sake of preaching on what I had meditated upon, but for the sake of obtaining food for my sou

It is vital that you as a church leader demonstrate a thirst for God's Word. It is vital that those in your church are daily drawn to its well of transformational power. It is vital that every believer thirsty for spiritual growth fights for time in the Scriptures and then feeds on its truths.

Jesus says in John 17:17: *Sanctify them by the truth; your word is truth.* Are you, the other leaders of your church, and your church congregation feeding your souls on the Living Word? If not, you are living life far from the richness of the transformed life.

- *God Uses Home and Family as Instruments of Growth.*

God uses the family unit as a cocoon for spiritual transformation. Cultivating such an environment not only gives children early glimpses of God's amazing love and strength, but it also provides fresh opportunities for you and others in your church to learn God's ways even as you seek to guide children (see Deut. 6:6-7). We are commanded to teach our children about God's commandments.

- *God Uses Believers to Help Others Grow to Be Like Jesus.*

Every believer being transformed by the work of the Holy Spirit is to help other believers grow to be more like Jesus. This is not an option for believers; it is a biblical mandate. *As iron sharpens iron, so one man sharpens another* (Prov. 27:17). Now read Ephesians 4:11-16. Believers, bonding together to challenge one another to become just like Jesus, represent one of God's most amazing transformational tools. How does one believer bond with other believers? One way is through group worship experiences. The unity of the spirit created through joint worship is reinforced by the person-to-person relationships that develop through church fellowship. The church is intended to be a place where all who walk through its doors know they have found true friends. *A friend loves at all times, and a brother is born for adversity* (Prov. 17:17). These friendships become even stronger through the nurturing bond of discipleship.

All the many gifts of the Spirit, all the many parts of the body of Christ, come together as one in the church. God intends for the church to be a powerful source of transformation for the believer. It is through a daily, intimate walk with Jesus that the people of the church come to know the heart of God. A church's organizations, structures, processes, procedures, and systems should ensure that they facilitate the Holy Spirit's work of spiritual transformation.

• *God Uses the Everyday Circumstances of Life.*

Life is filled with an abundance of unavoidable circumstances that cause pain—and an array of avoidable bad choices that necessitate discipline. God uses both circumstances and discipline to transform believers into His Son's likeness.

True spiritual transformation isn't without struggle; Jesus' life and death exemplify that. By trusting and obeying God in the midst of struggles, trying circumstances become a garden for heart-changing miracles.

In this you greatly rejoice, though now for a little while, you may have had to suffer grief in all kinds of trials. These have come so that your faith— of greater worth than gold, which perishes even though refined by fire—may be proved genuine and may result in praise, glory and honor when Jesus Christ is revealed (1 Pet. 1:6-7). Also see Romans 8:28,31b-32,37-39.

Yes, there are unavoidable circumstances—and we believers also pile grief on our own heads. During times when we make bad choices, God uses loving discipline to prune and shape us. While discipline often incurs acute loss, what we lose pales in comparison to gaining the wisdom and heart of Jesus. *Discipline....produces a harvest of righteousness and peace for those who have been trained by it* (Heb. 12:10-11).

• *God Uses Spiritual Exercises to Develop Growth.*

Bible study, prayer, fasting, and worship, are important for spiritual transformation. God will use almost any activity as a training exercise for spiritual transformation. The key to remember is that the activity is not intended to gauge spirituality but to create an avenue that God can use to lead believers straight to His heart. Spiritual exercises make us grow in our love for Him and for all people (see 1 Tim. 4:7b-8).

What Evidence of Spiritual Growth Does God Expect in a Believer's Life?
The measure of discipleship is how much a believer is like Jesus. Let's look at the things that reflect a transformed heart—for it is by mirroring the heart of God that believers glorify God. *God has chosen to make known among the Gentiles the glorious riches of this mystery, which is Christ in you, the hope of glory* (Col. 1:27).

• ***The Life of the Transformed Believer Models Love, Trust, and Obedience.***

Transformation of a believer's character will be evidenced by responding to the demands and events of life in the same character and manner as Jesus. *"Whoever has my commands and obeys them, he is the one who loves me. He who loves me will be loved by my Father, and I too will love him and show myself to him"* (John 14:21).

At the core of spiritual transformation rests this truth: Love and trust result in obedience. Obedience in a believer's relationship with Jesus produces even greater love and stronger faith. That doesn't imply that obedience is always easy. Obedience certainly wasn't easy for Jesus as the dark shadow of the cross inched ever closer to Him. Without Jesus' obedience, the world would have been lost. Without the obedience of believers, the church is just a social center. (See 1 John 5:2-5.)

• ***The Transformed Believer Lives in Harmony with God's Word.***

For believers, transformation is walking His Words, day in and day out, not just talking them. It's living God's Word out loud. Transformed believers live the Word of God and thus love God and others the way Jesus loves them. Fruit then is produced—not because of who is watching—but because of Who is guiding the actions. *"This is to my Father's glory, that you bear much fruit, showing yourselves to be my disciples"* (John 15:8).

In Matthew 11:28-30 Jesus says, *"Come to me...learn from me...and you will find rest for your souls."* The believer in the process of being transformed comes to God's Word for the wisdom and sustenance found there. The question, "How will this affect my relationship with Jesus?" becomes the lens through which believers look at every aspect of life.

• ***The Transformed Believer Sees the World Through the Lens of Scripture.***

God calls believers to see the world as Jesus did—to love the lost as

He does. God calls us to share His love with others. Transformed believers seize God-given opportunities to make a difference in the world.

With the lens of Scripture focusing our lives, things take on a clear perspective. Fear about spreading the gospel is replaced by a fervency to do so. Casual Christianity is replaced by commitment. Making a mere appearance in the world does not suffice; making a difference in the world, just as Jesus did, becomes the primary goal. *Finally, brothers, whatever is true, whatever is noble, whatever is right, whatever is pure, whatever is lovely, whatever is admirable—if anything is excellent or praiseworthy—think about such things. Whatever you have learned or received or heard from me, or seen in me—put it into practice. And the God of peace will be with you* (Phil. 4:8-9).

• *The Transformed Believer Has a Relationship with Other Believers.*

The Holy Spirit draws people of all different personalities, perspectives, and gifts together into a distinct and dedicated relationship with God, united as one spiritual family (the church) for His possession, use, and glory. These many believers are given different gifts by God so that the work of ministry may be accomplished efficiently. All believers have one calling—to glorify Him.

May the God who gives endurance and encouragement give you a spirit of unity among yourselves as you follow Christ Jesus, so that with one heart and mouth you may glorify the God and Father of our Lord Jesus Christ. Accept one another, then, just as Christ accepted you, in order to bring praise to God (Rom. 15:5-7).

The visibly transformed heart hears this ultimate calling to glorify God and reaches out to join hands with other believers, regardless of the differences they may have. Such a heart cultivates unity in the body of Christ by praying for other Christians, by avoiding gossip, by building others up, by working together in humility, by exalting Christ, and by refusing to get sidetracked arguing over details. It is a peaceful heart, not a warring one. It is a heart like the heart of Jesus. (See Phil. 2:1-6.)

• *The Transformed Believer Makes God's Love Known to Others.*

A transformed believer's love for God is reflected in loving people so much that the believer is compelled to make God's love known.

"Therefore, go and make disciples of all nations, baptizing them in the name of the Father and of the Son and of the Holy Spirit, teaching them to obey everything I have commanded you. And surely I am with you always, to the very end of the age" (Matt. 28:19-20).

God gives the transformed believer a new heart that propels him to reach out to the lost. Just as Jesus dedicated His life to making disciples, the transformed believer is dedicated to making disciples who, in turn, make more disciples. God's good, pleasing, and perfect will is that the believer become like Jesus and make the love of God known to others (see Rom. 12:1-2).

What Are the Hindrances to Spiritual Transformation?
Standing in the way of believers who want to become like Jesus are strong, well-trained opponents. So how does the believer prepare for this spiritual warfare? Understanding an enemy's "war chest" is the first step toward defeating an enemy. Understanding Satan's threats to spiritual transformation—specifically and intentionally arming oneself in preparation for the enemy's onslaughts—is the way to overcome them.

• *The Warfare of Satan.*
A tiny fawn was spotted standing alone. Unfortunately, three dogs also spotted the solitary creature and began vigorous pursuit. The dogs closed the distance. Suddenly, a person—intent on helping the fawn—ran screaming and yelling like a warrior after the dogs. They recognized a stronger opponent and quickly ran away. The tiny fawn, though bleeding slightly, ran into the woods toward its mother and safety.[10]

The story of the fawn parallels the believer's battle with Satan—and it emphasizes why the church must be so intentional in discipleship ministry. Just as the dogs targeted the solitary fawn, Satan attacks the most vulnerable believer and often the stronger leader—with full force. This can be a believer who separates himself from the church, a new believer, one whom the church fails to disciple and nurture into its protective fold, or a mature Christian who becomes overly self-reliant, complacent, or isolated.

When a believer stands alone, Satan always attacks. And Satan doesn't fight fair. You see, Satan cringes at the thought of believers becoming like Jesus. Satan works hard at halting your transformation journey. He knows the weaknesses of Christians—and he knows the most vulnerable time to send in the dogs. That's why Satan is such a huge hindrance to spiritual transformation. He is keen, he is vicious, and he has no mercy.

But for all of Satan's scheming to win battles, God has already won the war. Satan is powerless against Him. Jesus proclaimed in John 14:30-31, *"I will not speak with you much longer, for the prince of this world is coming. He has no hold on me, but the world must learn that I love the Father and that I do exactly what my Father has commanded me."* Even

Satan's ultimate scheme—the use of human leaders and systems to condemn Jesus to death—only resulted in the witness of God's eternal love for us and Jesus' total obedience.

Believers have the same power to defeat Satan because of our new identity in Christ. Even though we live in a battle zone as we journey toward spiritual transformation, the victory is ours because of Whose we are (the children of God) and who we are in Christ (joint heirs with Christ), complete with His spiritual DNA. What is required of us is:

- a constant, intentional desire to become like Jesus,
- a constant awareness of the schemes of Satan,
- a consistent faith that God will provide us with the strength to overpower Satan if we call upon Him,
- an ever-present willingness to bond with other believers for the battle, and
- a realization that God may discipline a believer in the process.

These five things require proactive intent. Intentional discipleship includes being acutely aware of our own vulnerable flanks and those of others. What are our vulnerable flanks? Individual weaknesses, destructive habits, and demonstrated strongholds in our lives that make us susceptible to attacks from Satan. These can include everything from addiction to alcohol, drugs, and pornography to eating disorders, poor self-esteem, or unbridled anger. The list is endless but not invincible.

Spiritual warfare is one area where the church is so vital to the transformation process. The body of Christ must be constantly vigilant and ever protective of those in its family—from the new Christian battling life-long addictions to the older Christian battling indifference.

You see, the church is filled with believers who have known both the agony of being attacked by Satan and the thrill of victory with Christ. It is also filled with believers who have relied on the strong, extended arms of other Christians when their own strength failed them.

Proverbs 18:24b says, *There is a friend who stands closer than a brother.* The body of Christ is that strong friend who helps fight battles and sustain weakened believers under attack from Satan. As believers seeking transformation, we must arm ourselves—not only for our own personal battles but to also help others fight their battles. Through intentional discipleship training, ministry opportunities, prayer linkages, worship experiences, sound biblical teaching, and intervention, the church becomes the primary conduit through which God works to fortify believers and make them more like His Son.

God gives believers strength for the journey, and there is comfort in knowing that other believers are there on the journey to provide encouragement, caution, wisdom, support, and when necessary, correction. The embattled believer then is never alone—even if Satan tries to convince him otherwise. Prepare in advance to battle Satan's onslaughts with the armor of daily prayer, reading of God's Word, and the help of other believers. This strong, steady armor is necessary for the spiritual transformation journey.

Your enemy the devil prowls around like a roaring lion looking for someone to devour. Resist him, standing firm in the faith, because you know that your brothers throughout the world are undergoing the same kind of sufferings. And the God of all grace, who called you to his eternal glory in Christ, after you have suffered a little while, will himself restore you and make you strong, firm and steadfast (1Pet. 5: 8-10). See also 2 Timothy 4:16-18a and Romans 16:20.

• ***The Ways of the World.***

Believers face temptation to conform to the world's perspective every day. The temptation to conform to the world is marketed well—abortion as choice, lust as freedom of expression, and greed as determination. Each believer must develop a keen eye for God's truth and then stand his or her ground against the world often feeling alone against the masses. The struggle can be exhausting (1 John 2:15-16). But for all the clever marketing the world does, the difference between the world and the Father are clear when God's Word is used as a lens. Jesus said, *"Take heart! I have overcome the world"* (John 16:33).

• ***The War Against Self.***

While the believer receives a new spiritual DNA from Christ with repentance and salvation, the old self-centered nature is still hanging around. It engages the believer in a spiritual war against God-centeredness. *So then, I myself in my mind am a slave to God's law, but in the sinful nature a slave to the law of sin* (Rom. 7:25).

This battle against oneself can be fierce. The transformed believer must stay focused on Jesus to overpower the pull of self-centeredness. A heart like His doesn't ask, "What do I get?" It asks, "What can I give?" It doesn't demand, "Satisfy me!" It says, "Not my will but Yours." The believer is empowered to lay down personal desires and to follow God's will, just as Jesus did. *"I have come down from heaven not to do my will but to do the will of him who sent me"* (John 6:38).

• *Lack of Faith.*

When the road to spiritual transformation becomes steep often the believer must battle a lack of faith, which is usually based in fear. Fear can stop the believer in his tracks. Though the journey to spiritual transformation may be steep and treacherous at times, fear can be overcome by an abiding faith and the heart-felt knowledge that Jesus is there to lead the way. The journey is never a solo one. The Bible says, *"Do not let your hearts be troubled. Trust in God; trust also in me"* (John 14:1). *"I tell you the truth, anyone who has faith in me will do what I have been doing. He will do even greater things"* (John 14:12). *For everyone born of God overcomes the world. This is the victory that has overcome the world, even our faith* (1 John 5:4).

• *Lack of Knowledge and Understanding.*

Ignorance of God's Word is a huge barrier to a growing relationship with Jesus Christ. The battle for the mind is a struggle between thinking and acting God's way—by faith—as opposed to thinking and operating by man's limited ability to reason.

In Proverbs 3:5-6, we see the importance of studying the Word of God. *Trust in the Lord with all your heart and lean not on your own understanding; in all your ways acknowledge him, and he will make your paths straight.*

Hosea 4:6a reveals what happens when a believer relies on his own limited ability to reason. *"My people are destroyed from lack of knowledge."* Shallow biblical knowledge leaves the believer vulnerable to attacks by Satan. Satan plants weeds of misinformation in a field of truth. The unprepared believer can be choked by Satan's weeds without even knowing it. The prepared believer is safeguarded by a full knowledge of the new identity possessed in Christ. A mind built up on the Scriptures is a mind focused on becoming like Jesus.

"For I gave them the words you gave me and they accepted them…Sanctify them by the truth; your word is truth" (John 17:8,17). *You have known the holy Scriptures, which are able to make you wise for salvation through faith in Christ Jesus. All Scripture is God-breathed and is useful for teaching, rebuking, correcting and training in righteousness, so that the man of God may be thoroughly equipped for every good work* (2 Tim. 3:14-17).

• *The Dangerous Drift.*

One of the most subtle hindrances to becoming like Jesus is the unintentional detour that can leave a believer's life stranded. Satan loves it when believers drift away, clueless as to what's happening. He nods and waves as a believer drifts by and is immensely pleased.

The Bible says to *pay careful attention* against drifting because it can happen subtly (Heb. 2:1). It happens most often when a believer gets lazy with his or her prayer life and Bible study—or too busy with daily life. The believer can drift away from God's will and be unaware of it until there's a jolt—a personal crisis, a concerned friend's confrontation, discipline from God. A drifting believer is in spiritual limbo—they no longer *grow in the grace and knowledge of our Lord and Savior Jesus Christ* (2 Pet. 3:18). When growth stops, susceptibility to sin increases.

• *Rebellion.*

A rebellious heart is a far graver matter for a believer. The believer chooses to turn his back on spiritual growth. The overtness of rebellion is like a fist in the face of God. The Bible spotlights the pain and unhappiness that surrounded the Israelites when they shook their fists in God's face and said, "We want it our way!" They got what their fists asked for—God's wrath and discipline. *"Today, if you hear his voice, do not harden your hearts as you did in the rebellion"* (Heb. 3:15).

A believer who chooses to rebel against God—to replace love, trust, and obedience with a self-centered will—is destined for hard times. Saying "No!" to God wreaked havoc in Jonah's life—Jonah learned the hard, way, that you can't run from God, and you can't say you love God if you aren't willing to do what He asks. *"He who does not love me will not obey my teaching"* (John 14:24). *They stumble because they disobey the message—which is also what they were destined for* (1 Pet. 2:8).

Rebellion barricades the believer from God's best—and creates messy consequences that can last a lifetime. But repentance and forgiveness brings rebellious believers like Jonah back on track, capable of accomplishing great things for God's glory. Rebellion gets the believer in a whale of a mess every time. Going forward with God always brings peace and joy.

• *Distraction.*

One of the most effective hindrances Satan uses against believers is distraction. Satan can veer the believer from a growing personal relationship with Jesus to activities that may or may not be good things. He can distract the believer from victory in Jesus to fears about the future and regrets about the past. He can turn a heart from the grace and mercy of Christ to legalistic self-righteousness, from focus on God's glory to the pursuit of personal ambition, from character-based spiritual transformation to activity-based performance. The list is endless and dangerous. The Bible says the believer's eyes should be focused on Jesus Himself at all times. Nothing must distract the believer from making Jesus the center of his or her life. *"No one who puts his hand to the plow and looks back is fit for service in the kingdom of God"* (Luke 9:62).

The Role of the Church in Transformation
We cannot emphasize enough the importance of being prepared to do battle as you journey toward spiritual transformation. Paul admonishes the church to never underestimate the strength of Satanic warfare and the many hindrances to spiritual transformation. Eugene Peterson's paraphrase, *The MESSAGE*, sums it up this way in Ephesians 6:10-18: *"God is strong, and he wants you strong. So take everything the Master has set out for you, well-made weapons of the best materials. And put them to use so you will be able to stand up to everything the Devil throws your way. This is no afternoon athletic contest that we'll walk away from and forget about in a couple of hours. This is for keeps, a life-or-death fight to the finish against the Devil and all his angels.*

Be prepared. You're up against far more than you can handle on your own. Take all the help you can get, every weapon God has issued, so that when it's all over but the shouting you'll still be on your feet. Truth, righteousness, peace, faith, and salvation are more than words. Learn how to apply them. You'll need them throughout your life. God's Word is an indispensable weapon. In the same way, prayer is essential in this ongoing warfare. Pray hard and long. Pray for your brothers and sisters. Keep your eyes open. Keep each other's spirits up so that no one falls behind or drops out."

"Press on" Paul says in Philippians 4:13. **The church is called to cultivate an environment to help the believer press on toward becoming like Jesus.**

GET THIS ⇨ *The heart of this chapter…*
Spiritual transformation is God's work of changing a believer into the likeness of Jesus by creating a new identity in Christ and by empowering a lifelong relationship of love, trust, and obedience to glorify God. It is a God-empowered miracle; it cannot emerge from human effort.

GET PERSONAL ⇨ *How this applies to you and your church…*
How does knowing you have the spiritual DNA of Jesus change your perception of yourself and your perception of your church's potential for ministry?

Is your personal relationship with Jesus closer today than it was this time last year?

Do you sense such a growing relationship in the other leaders of your church? In the members of your church?

What are three priority actions you can do in your church during the next six months to build awareness of spiritual transformation?

What are two creative ways you can restructure worship services and church curriculum to help the church body recognize and maximize the real-life resources God uses to transform them into the likeness of Jesus?

How can you communicate to your church body the tangible things that evidence spiritual transformation in a believer's life?

What barriers can you identify that could be preventing individuals from experiencing spiritual transformation?

List some "body guards" your church can begin to incorporate into its structure during the next six months to help believers recognize and overcome the hindrances to spiritual transformation.

GET GOING ⇨ *Tips for proactive discipleship…*
1. Encourage individual and group studies of the book *Jesus By Heart*, which guides the believer through the spiritual transformation process.

2. Incorporate the goal of loving, trusting, and obeying as Jesus did into the vision and mission statements of your church. How will this impact the way you "do church" and the way you and others in your church reach out to your community?

3. What specific things is your church currently doing to create an environment that helps believers love, trust, and obey as Jesus did? What things are you not doing now that you can begin doing within the next six months?

4. Over a period of several weeks, ask groups of deacons, Sunday School teachers, committee chairpersons, ministry leaders, or church staff mem-

bers to (a) list the spiritually-based activities they are involved in; (b) evaluate on a scale of 1 to 5 how each activity helped people develop a personal relationship to God; (c) ask them to estimate how much time the people involved in these activities spend developing their personal relationship with God; (d) ask them what could be different in the activities, if the goal were to spiritually transform lives. (Refer to pp. 25-26.); (e) ask them if their relationship with Jesus is closer today than last month or last year; (f) ask them if the leaders and members' relationship to Christ is growing (Refer to pp. 27-28.); (g) in a group setting ask them to make up their churches "to do" list. Lead them to pray that they would crave a relationship with Him more than any "to do" list. Be sensitive as to who you involve. You are looking to revitalize your church. Involve people who will join you in the journey. It may take several groups over a period of time.

5. Get a group of church leaders to join you in studying John 13-14 (refer to p. 26).

6. With this same group ask a heart surgeon, or a person who has experienced heart surgery to describe the purpose and process. Ask a health, exercise, or physical therapist to describe the processes needed to improve or change a heart. Using the information on pages 27-28 lead the group to study spiritual transformation. Talk about how your church can lead people to experience spiritual transformation.

7. Consider making spiritual transformation a major two- or three-month emphasis in your church, revisiting your church's mission statement to include spiritual transformation, and praying about spiritual transformation becoming a life and ministry objective.

8. Have *Jesus By Heart* and *My Identity in Christ* small-group studies available for every one in your church.

9. Ask the groups to discuss and evaluate the five resources (1. Living Word; 2. Family; 3. Believers; 4. Everyday Circumstances; 5. Spiritual Exercises.) identified on pages 30-32 that God uses to transform lives. Ask them to rate how each of these resources is effective in your church to transform lives. Then ask them to discuss ways to improve these resources to be more effective in spiritual transformation.

10. Ask a group of Sunday School teachers how thirsty their class is for the Word of God.

11. Invite "Spiritual Lighthouses" in your church to share testimonies of their Bible study or a spiritual truth they just learned in their quiet time.

12. Ask parents to share a testimony of how they want to be used and available to lead spiritual transformation in their home. Ask a mature teenager to share how their family shapes their spiritual life. Have families demonstrate family Bible study in a worship service.

13. Share testimonies of how other believers helped them grow to be like Jesus. Share note cards with the congregation and ask them to write a thank you note to someone who helped show them to be like Jesus.

14. Ask individuals to share testimonies of how God used circumstances to transform believers into His likeness.

15. Of the spiritual exercises listed on page 31, which ones have been most utilized in your life or in your church to lead people to be like Jesus? Which ones are new resources of spiritual exercise.

16. With a group of church leaders, ask them to look again at the church calendar for the next several months. Ask the question, How will these activities affect the individual's in our church and their relationship with Jesus. (Refer to p. 32 for the question.)

17. List the hindrances found on pp. 34-39. Rank them in order according to the greatest to the least hindrance for your church in the next one-to-three years. List things you think might be done either to do away with the hindrances or to improve the situation in your church. Who in your church needs to be praying about these hindrances?

[9]George Muller. *Soul Nourishment First* (Los Angeles: Bible House of Los Angeles, 1900).
[10]Adapted from *Home Again* © by Ivey Harrington. Used by permission.

WHAT GOD WANTS HIS CHURCH TO "GET"

Oz Guinness tells the following story in his book *The Call:*

"Arthur F. Burns, the chairman of the United States Federal Reserve System and ambassador to West Germany, was a man of considerable gravity. Medium in height, distinguished, with wavy silver hair and his signature pipe, he was economic counselor to numerous presidents from Dwight D. Eisenhower to Ronald Reagan. When he spoke, his opinion carried weight and Washington listened.

"Arthur Burns was also Jewish, so when he began attending an informal White House group for prayer and fellowship in the 1970s, he was accorded special respect. No one in fact knew quite how to involve him in the group and, week after week when different people took turns to end the meeting in prayer, Burns was passed by—out of a mixture of respect and reticence.

"One week, however, the group was led by a newcomer who did not know the unusual status Burns occupied. As the meeting ended, the newcomer turned to Arthur Burns and asked him to close the time with a prayer. Some of the old-timers glanced at each other in surprise and wondered what would happen. But without missing a beat, Burns reached out, held hands with the others in the circle, and prayed this prayer: 'Lord, I pray that you would bring Jews to know Jesus Christ. I pray that you would bring Muslims to know Jesus Christ. Finally, Lord, I pray that you would bring Christians to know Jesus Christ. Amen.'

"Arthur Burns's prayer has become legendary in Washington. Not only did he startle those present with his refreshing directness, but he also underscored a point about 'Christians' and 'Christianity' that needs repeating regularly. It highlights an important aspect of the truth of calling: *Calling reminds Christians ceaselessly that, far from having arrived, a Christian is someone who in this life is always on the road as 'a follower of Christ' and a follower of 'the Way.'"*[11]

Given this clear individual calling for each Christian, it stands to reason that the church's primary calling is inextricably linked to helping Christians follow Christ and become like Him. To put it simply: Jesus is in the business of changing selfish people into servant leaders, and the church's role is to create a warm, nurturing environment that fosters this miraculous metamorphosis.

Does such a spiritual environment exist at your church? Think back

> God is waiting for the church to lay its to-do-lists at His feet, seek His face, and abide in Him.

through the minutes of recent business meetings. What core values are reflected in the decisions made at those meetings? Does discipleship permeate their fiber? Is it the core value that directs the functions of your church? Are you and other church leaders becoming more like Jesus every day? Is your church nurturing its people to become more like Jesus? If not, why not?

The joyful (and indeed miraculous) truth is this: God can transform not only you but other church leaders and every member of your church to be like His Son Jesus. In fact, He has called the church to spiritual transformation, and He has made the message and the method clear in 2 Corinthians 3:18 and Romans 12:1-2:

And we, who with unveiled faces all reflect the Lord's glory, are being transformed into his likeness, with ever-increasing glory, which comes from the Lord, who is the Spirit (2 Cor. 3:18). *Therefore, I urge you, brothers, in view of God's mercy, to offer your bodies as living sacrifices, holy and pleasing to God—this is your spiritual act of worship. Do not conform any longer to the pattern of this world, but be transformed by the renewing of your mind. Then you will be able to test and approve what God's will is—his good, pleasing and perfect will* (Rom. 12:1-2).

Are you and the other believers in your church in *God's good, pleasing and perfect will*? Are you focused on becoming like Jesus? Your church can be. It should be. It must be. The very heart of God is that believers be transformed into the likeness of His Son. By coming to know Jesus, believers come to know God.

If there is any fog about God's intention for the church, Jesus clears it in John 14:6-7 by clarifying that an intimate, heart-to-heart relationship with Jesus is not only the key to spiritual health but also the direct line to God Himself. In fact, it's the only link to God. *"I am the way and the truth and the life. No one comes to the Father except through me. If you really knew me, you would know my Father as well. From now on you do know him and have seen him."* You, the leaders in your church, and the members of your congregation must commit yourselves to really *know* Jesus personally.

The question that has baffled so many Christians: "What would God have me do with my life now that I've repented of my sins and trusted Jesus?" has been answered. You, the other leaders of your church, and the believers who worship are to become like Jesus so that others may come to know Him personally and grow to be like Him. Any other goal or accomplishment in a believer's life, or your church's life, should spring from this core purpose and relationship.

The call of God is simple: "Be like My Son, Jesus." The directive is so simple, so clearly stated in Scripture, that it is perplexing that the church has been slow to embrace transformational discipleship as its core value.

As a leader in your church, it's vital that you embrace this core value of discipleship and centralize your own relationship with Jesus, just as Frank Laubach did. The discipleship ministry of your church will never rise any higher than its leaders' heart for spiritual transformation; therefore, it is vital that you model for the church leaders and those in the congregation that Jesus is the "main thing." Then, as a church leader, it is vital your church model transformational discipleship—nurturing other believers toward becoming like Jesus. Otherwise, transformational discipleship will just exist as one more emphasis or segmented program on your church's docket. And a church that has lost its zeal for discipleship has lost its focus on its main, God-directed mission.

How do you begin such a discipleship focus? By passing every program, every ministry opportunity through a simple filter: **Will this particular ministry help me and my church become more like Jesus?**

Why is this filter so crucial to the health of your church? For a church to be healthy, the individuals in it must be spiritually healthy. That requires individuals to have a personal relationship with Jesus as their core value. Without this core relationship, the pursuit of spiritual growth becomes activity-based performance rather than character-based spiritual transformation. And only internal transformation produces dramatic behavioral changes that glorify God.

In his book, *The Antioch Effect*, Ken Hemphill makes a crucial diagnostic point, "Healthy churches place a high priority on promoting the growth of people toward Christlikeness, which is the fundamental issue of the discipling ministry of the church."[12]

As we define discipleship for the new millennium, Hemphill has clearly echoed what Jesus said in Matthew 28:19-20. *"Therefore go and make disciples of all the nations, baptizing them in the name of the Father and of the Son and of the Holy Spirit, and teaching them to obey everything I have commanded you. And surely I am with you always, to the very end of the age."*

The Greek grammar used in this passage is insightful as we think about the impact of the words of Jesus. There is only one imperative — the rest of the verb forms are participles. The only actual command is to "make disciples." There is no imperative command to go, to baptize, or to teach. Those are merely methods we are to use in fulfilling the command to make disciples. Thus this Scripture is more accurately translated "as you are going, make disciples—baptizing and teaching them."

Scripture then is clear: Discipleship is the primary mandate of the church, not as a program, but as an essential ingredient in transforming lives. As we make this strong statement, we are not compromising the truth of God's Word but intentionally evaluating the methodology of how discipleship takes place. You see, transformational discipleship stands in sharp contrast to spiritual growth methods that focus on absorbing information about the Christian life or on performing acts of service and ministry or on organizing activities for church members. Although believers should look for opportunities to grow and serve, neither knowledge nor service is the test of discipleship. The path to true transformational discipleship, the path to guiding those in your church to experiencing God face-to-face, can only be traveled by obediently coming to know Jesus. That's why Jesus took His twelve disciples with Him wherever He went. He wanted them to experience Him and by doing so, experience God Himself. Jesus did not sit and teach the disciples about the Father. He helped them intimately *know* the Father.

Think about that: to intimately *know* the Father. As a spiritual leader do you help the people of your church *know* the Father? Do they experience Him because of walking with you?

In our generation, we feel, or so it seems, that we can just teach a Sunday School lesson and class members will leave knowing God. But they won't. They may leave knowing more *about* God, but that doesn't mean they've personally *experienced* Him in their lives. If we as church leaders can help those in our churches come to really know and experience and walk with the Father, just as Jesus helped His disciples do, no doubt about it, lives will be transformed and God will be glorified.

Remember, we are not just talking about teaching a Sunday School class or facilitating a small group. We are not talking about just packing the pews every Sunday either. Neither are we talking about reaching out to the needy. **We are talking about walking with a group of people until they have personally experienced God.** That is true discipleship. That is transformational discipleship. And that is God's mandate for the church. If people are walking with Him, the ministry and leadership needs of a church will take care of itself, because as people grow they want to get in on what God is doing.

The Quandary of the Millennium Church

For a moment let's ponder two paths to spiritual growth: face-to-face relationship versus cerebral knowledge. Here lies the quandary of the millennium church. We've weighted the cerebral far more than the relational. And it is evident in the frantic activity-based life of the church that our heads are out-talking our hearts. Are we being transformed by God or merely remodeled by activities driven by man?

Sadly, the average Christian has extensive head knowledge about God but doesn't really *know* God well enough to believe Him when He gives a directive in life. Every time God comes to guide in a specific direction, Christians struggle against Him because they don't fully trust this Stranger in their midst. That's one of the reasons this world and our nation are in the shape they're in—God's people don't know Him; as a result, they don't obey Him.

If a greater number of God's people really knew God personally—not just cerebrally—and obeyed everything He was telling them, we would see revival in our lives, our churches, our nation, and our world. Make no mistake, it is the responsibility of spiritual leaders like yourself to cultivate an environment in your church that nurtures believers to a face-to-face, heart-to-heart relationship with God. Head knowledge about God is merely an indent in the cerebral cortex that can produce spiritual activity on the outside. Relationship with God is a heart transplant that forever changes lives.

You see, as church leaders, we've been given a serious responsibility. God is holding the church responsible to make sure that the outer activity of believers is a reflection of inner reality; otherwise, it is simply a lot of handclapping and backpatting. In Matthew 6:1, Jesus firmly warns the church about activity-based Christianity. *"Be careful not to do your 'acts of righteousness' before men, to be seen by them. If you do, you will have no reward from your Father in heaven."*

The MESSAGE paraphrases it this way: *"Be especially careful when you are trying to be good so that you don't make a performance out of it. It might be good theater, but the God who made you won't be applauding."*

No, God does not reward to-do lists and linear stepping-stones to spiritual growth. What He does reward, what He sent Jesus to model, is internal character-change—not external, activity-based momentum. The essence of God-empowered spiritual transformation is that, as believers, our actual character will reflect the same character and manner of Jesus in responding to the demands, events, aggravations, and challenges of life. Granted, following Jesus' example is difficult, but the Scriptures promise it is totally achievable through the work of the Holy Spirit in our lives.

Here is the truth of the matter: **God gives the church great flexibility in the *way* it does things—but not in *what* it does.** The words of Jesus in Matthew 28 make the mission of the church clear: The responsibility for discipling rests with the church and all believers. In other words, your church is given the instruction to take the spiritual initiative for cultivating an environment of love, trust, and obedience to God, all for His glory. It is not an environment that pushes cataclysm—sudden or drastic change in lives—but instead one that nurtures the transformation of believers from man's nature into God's nature. The following story illustrates the difference between forcing cataclysm and nurturing spiritual transformation.

One day I (Barry) noticed a cocoon hanging on a branch. As I watched, the encased butterfly struggled to force its way through a tiny hole. After several hours the butterfly seemed to stop making progress. So I decided to help the butterfly carefully snipping off the remaining cocoon. The butterfly then emerged easily, but it had a swollen body and small, shriveled wings. I watched the butterfly because I expected that, at any moment, the wings would enlarge and expand to be able to support the swollen body. Neither happened, the butterfly spent the rest of its short life crawling around with a swollen body and shriveled wings. It was never able to fly and it never became a thing of beauty.

What I didn't understand was the butterfly's struggle to get through the tiny opening in the cocoon was God's way of slowly forcing fluid from its body into its wings so that it would be ready for flight once freedom was achieved. I prevented this gradual transformational process.

Likewise, the church must not force dramatic change on believers, suddenly thrust them into spiritual activities, or expect them to run spiritually before they've learned to crawl. Instead, as people are freed from the cocoon of sin and enter into a personal relationship with Jesus, it is the church's responsibility to support and assist the work of the Holy Spirit by nurturing the believer. A healthy, growing, and vibrant church will recognize its God-given responsibility to slowly nurture emerging believers and it will develop a discipleship ministry conducive to this.

Jesus was and is in the business of slowly transforming self-centered people into servant-centered people. Not for the sake of "finding God" but for the sake of "knowing God" through Him. When the church grasps this concept and becomes an instrument God can use to make disciples, two wonderful things happen: Christians become spiritually healthy and God will pull others toward Himself through them.

How do you as a church leader guide the believers in your congregation to truly know God, to transition from head-knowledge of Him to heart-to-heart intimacy with Him? Believers are transformed by keeping their focus on Jesus. Granted, the process of refocusing may be a bit awkward at times—focus shifts almost always are.

Likewise, you as a church leader will encounter some spiritual turbulence if you choose to personally navigate the transformational journey and shepherd others toward transformation. Most people don't like to experience change. Change makes them uncomfortable, irritable, or appear mean. We don't have to explain that to you. As a church leader you've lived it. We've lived it, too, so we can empathize with how you may feel as you contemplate a new church focus. However, the Bible promises you this: Through the relationship of love, trust, and obedience that Jesus modeled, God will carry you and your church to the proper destination—regardless of the turbulence. The rewards that come from refocusing yourself, as well as others, on becoming like Jesus are nothing short of miraculous.

A New Perspective

About now you may be feeling that uncomfortable twinge in whatever part of your body you store stress. Relax and know this: **A refocus of your church on transformational discipleship doesn't require that you start from scratch with an entirely new church program. It only requires that you look at your church's ministries, programs, and emphasis with a new perspective. The perspective of Jesus.** Your church is about the business of reaching people, leading them to spiritual transformation, which always results in their finding their own personal ministry in their church, home, school, work, and community.

The wonderful truth is, rather than make your church's path more complex, focusing on transformational discipleship will simplify the life of your church. You will find your church accomplishes more for God because less energy will be siphoned away by activity-based programs that do not help you and your congregation become more like Jesus. A church focused on transformational discipleship is a church focused on Jesus. As a church leader, as a believer, can you think of a better focal point?

Testing 1. 2. 3.

Jesus came to earth to show us what God is like, to restore our relationship with God through His sacrificial death on the cross, and to model for believers a life that is pleasing to God. From the life of Jesus, we can discern three key characteristics of a disciple. Consider this three-point discipleship test. Do you have…

1. An abiding relationship with God?
2. A Christ-centered relationship with the body (the church)?
3. A broadening God-directed impact on the world?

Well? Not sure? The following questions will help you and other church leaders reflect on and evaluate your current relationships with God:

• Are my thoughts, attitudes, and actions becoming more like Jesus?
• Does more than 30 minutes pass without my thinking about Jesus?
• Do I eagerly seek opportunities to worship and praise God?
• Do I eagerly seek prayer and Bible study times?
• How do I handle difficult situations that require sacrifice?
• How do I deal with trials?

These next questions will help you and other church leaders reflect on and evaluate your relationship with believers (the church):

• To what degree do I love my brothers and sisters in Christ?
• To what degree do I love those that are difficult to love?
• How do I respond to conflict with another believer?
• How quickly do I forgive?
• Am I bothered by immature Christians?

These final questions will lead you and other church leaders to reflect on your relationship to the world:

• To what degree do I love the lost?
• In the way I spend my day, does it reflect Christ with integrity, commitment, joy, and accountability?
• How am I influencing those around me?
• Do I invest my resources in expanding God's kingdom?
• How is our church transforming the culture?
• How are our church members living their faith and impacting the culture?

Jesus modeled how we should live as Christians reflecting His image. The scriptural directive then is clear: Learning to live, love, trust, and obey as Jesus did—and helping others do the same is God's purpose for the church. This is the key to living in God's *"good, pleasing, and per-*

fect will." Moreover, shepherding your church through this type of life-change is simply a matter of refocusing—not on new church programs and models—but on Jesus and principle-centered discipleship—discipleship principles Jesus demonstrated every day of His life.

Principle Persuasion

If Jesus were to assess the complex church programs, methods, models, and techniques we use today, we think the first thing He would say would be, "You're making this far too hard."

You see, in training His disciples—and in living every aspect of His life on earth—"Jesus majored on principles rather than on methods. He concentrated on meeting the needs of people rather than on developing and imparting techniques. He spent His time developing sound thought processes rather than skills. And, most importantly, He taught by example how to trust God rather than teaching theories about God."[13]

That is how Jesus did life, isn't that how we should do it?

GET THIS ⇨ *The heart of this chapter…*

Jesus is in the business of changing selfish people into servant leaders, and the church's role is to create a warm, nurturing environment that fosters this miraculous metamorphosis. A church's organizations, structures, processes, procedures, and systems should ensure that they facilitate the Holy Spirit's work of spiritual transformation. Teaching others to love, trust, and obey as Jesus did is God's purpose for the church. All of this should be done to glorify God.

GET PERSONAL ⇨ *How this applies to you and your church…*

Evaluate the health and effectiveness of your church's current discipleship ministry.

• What percentage of people who are active in your church are currently involved in discipleship ministry?

• What percentage of those are experiencing spiritual transformation?

• Is discipleship contained within the large group of your church or does it permeate into small groups?

• In what ways are people experiencing true relationship, a sense of community, because of your current discipleship ministry?

• In what ways are you and others in your church becoming more like Jesus because of your current discipleship ministry? Which areas are lacking?

• How effectively is your church's current discipleship ministry training believers to meet the needs of a hurting society?

• How are new leaders being raised up through your current discipleship ministry?

Take the time to make a list of all of your church's programs and ministries.

• Where are your church's time, money, and efforts going? Ask yourself: What are we doing and why? For instance, look at the minutes of your last three years of business meetings/church counsel meetings—as well as your church budget and calendar. Based on these records, evaluate your church's priorities. (Do this in the proper spirit; this is not a time to point fingers or imply guilt. Instead, this is a time to evaluate the health of your church.)

Pass your church records through the following filter: How did this particular ministry/program, budget item, or event help me and my church become more like Jesus? This question will help you determine the strengths, weaknesses, and true purpose of each ministry, program, budgeted item, and church event. Write these down. The passing of each ministry or program through this filter will help determine which pursuits should be kept, discontinued, or need remodeling if they are to help you and your church become more like Jesus. Your assessment may also encourage you to develop entirely new ministries that are more clearly focused on discipleship.

• How can you shift your discipleship approach from teaching about the Father to bringing others face-to-face with Him? What specific things can you do to help other church leaders make this shift in perspective?

GET GOING ⇨ *Tips for proactive discipleship...*
1. Ask your church members to privately and anonymously write down what percent of the church attenders believe the church's primary calling is "linked to helping Christians follow Christ and become like Him." Have these numbers and ask the group to comment. Then ask them if this is an issue they need to pray, think about, and discuss. Ask them to think about how their church would be different if the average percentage grew. Discuss the questions starting on the bottom of page 43.
2. Study and memorize 2 Corinthians 3:18; Romans 12:1-2; John 14:6-7, and encourage your church to do so, too.

3. Encourage those you lead to take the activity test you took in this chapter, pages 50-51, and the three-point discipleship test on page 50. These thought-provoking questions will help individuals assess their balance between solitude with God and outward ministry activities, as well as the health of their heart for discipleship.

4. Encourage those you lead to write the following question in their daily planners on the first day of each week for the entire year. *Is my relationship with Jesus closer today than it was this time last week?* Confronting this question every week will help believers regularly assess their relationship with Jesus and set aside necessary time for adjustments when their daily planners are in their hands.

5. After evaluating the effectiveness of your current ministry, recruit a special team of prayer warriors to petition God for a church-wide burden for discipleship ministry. Encourage them to pray specifically for discipleship ministry leaders.

6. Build a strategy for your discipleship ministry. What does the end result look like? What is your vision/purpose? Based on the biblical principles of *Transformational Discipleship*, what would you hope your church looked like in two years? Five years? Ten years? What kinds of needs would be met? How would lives be "changed?" How would healthy and effective discipleship groups affect and support the other ministries of the church?

[11]Oz Guinness. *The Call, Finding and Fulfilling the Central Purpose of Your Life* (Nashville: Word Publishing, 1998), 106-107. All rights reserved. Used by permission.

[12]Ken Hemphill, *The Antioch Effect* (Nashville: Broadman and Holman Pub., 1994) 181. All rights reserved.

[13]Walter A. Henrichsen. *Disciples Are Made—Not Born* (Victor Books, a division of SP Publications, © 1974) 118-127. 1978.

IT HAS TO BE JESUS

The health of all other relationships is dependent upon an abiding relationship with Jesus.

> **The Relationship Principle:**
> Transformation takes place in relationships. Our relationship with Jesus is the foundational relationship that affects every other relationship in life.

An architect of a large bridge stated of the massive structure: "The bridge is totally preoccupied with the foundation."

What an incredible statement! It says everything about what life as a believer should be—totally preoccupied with the Foundation of faith—Jesus Christ. He is the Bridge that crosses the great divide between God and man.

From the Old Testament through the New, the Bible illustrates the importance of knowing God, of being preoccupied by that foundational relationship. But somehow today, it seems easy to gravitate from a heart-to-heart relationship with God to a cerebral one. Stop for a moment and imagine a game show in which the following question was asked:

"Who do you imagine knew the most about God…Abraham in the Old Testament or a modern-day theologian?"

Abraham could not have told you about the two advents of Christ; nor could he have explained the differences between the pre-, post-, and amillennial positions; nor could he have dialogued extensively on the duel nature of Christ, the virgin birth, nor a dozen other points of theology. But Abraham *knew* God! He has a singular place in Scripture as a man who pleased God. In the New Testament alone, he is mentioned 74 times. Let's look at two of those mentioned.

Abraham believed God, and it was accounted to him for righteousness (Gal. 3:6). That's a huge statement regarding Abraham's relationship with God. It signifies that Abraham was totally preoccupied with God. In fact, God was so pleased with this man that Hebrews 11:16 says, *God is not ashamed to be called their* [Abraham's] *God.* Think about what God was saying. It is one thing to be known by God. It is an entirely different relationship when the God of heaven and earth says, "I am the God of Abraham." What God is saying here is that the Creator is known by the creature—and God was proud to call Abraham His Own because Abraham's life helped others to know God.

Can the living God be known to others by you? Can God say, "If you want to know what I am like, look at the life of the person reading this book"? God said that about Jesus. Jesus reflected the heart of God because Jesus constantly abided with His Father in a relationship of love, trust, and obedience. That's the type of deep, abiding relationship God wants with you, and with us, and with every believer in your church.

Our relationship with Jesus, our deep, abiding relationship, determines how great our witness is to the world. In other words, a far-reaching witness requires a close-knit relationship with Jesus. You might also add that the health of all other relationships is dependent on an abiding relationship with Jesus. The most crucial aspect of spiritual transformation is an abiding, intimate, growing relationship with God.

The foundational principle of transformational discipleship is the relationship principle. The extent to which your church lives out of this principle is the extent to which spiritual transformation will occur. Helping every believer to understand how they are to abide in Christ is central to everything your church is and does.

If we look at the history of Israel, we discover that when the king had an intimate relationship with God—the nation prospered; but, when a king neglected his relationship with God—the nation suffered. The same can be said today of our relationships. Keep your and your church's primary focus on knowing and becoming like Jesus and all other relationships—marriage, family, friendships, church, work, acquaintances, community, and society—are encouraged to become more Christlike.

The legacy of this truth can be seen in Acts 6 when the apostles asked the church to appoint seven men full of the Holy Spirit, faith, and wisdom to take care of the heavy responsibility of the day-to-day needs of the people. What did the apostles do to fortify themselves for such a huge responsibility? They gave themselves continually *to prayer and the ministry of the word* (v. 4). It is obvious that the apostles knew that their personal relationship with Jesus was of utmost importance to the growth and health of the church. They made that relationship their priority. Jesus reaffirmed the importance of abiding with Christ as a condition for spiritual leadership in Acts 1:21-22. He chose to replace the betraying Judas with *one of the men who have been with us the whole time the Lord Jesus went in and out among us…from John's baptism to the time when Jesus was taken up from us.*

As the church leaders of today, it is vital that we emulate these apostles if we are to shepherd our churches toward spiritual transformation. In his sermon, "The Main Thing," the Rev. Pat Hood of the First Baptist Church in Smyrna, Tennessee, challenges church leaders to authenticity and first allegiance to God.

"A person can never lead anyone beyond where they are themselves. Therefore, if my staff and I desire to lead and challenge the believers in our church to soar to new heights in their relationships with Christ, we must let nothing interfere with our personal relationships with Jesus."[14]

Let nothing interfere—three powerful words that can change the entire life of your church. Let nothing interfere with your relationship with God, for it is the nucleus of health for all other relationships. This truth establishes why Jesus was so definitive when asked by the Pharisees *"Which is the greatest commandment?"*

"Love the Lord your God with all your heart and with all your soul and with all your mind. This is the first and greatest commandment. And the second is like it: 'Love your neighbor as yourself.' All the Law and the Prophets hang on these two commandments" (Matt. 22:37-40).

The entire process of transformational discipleship hinges on these two relational truths. First, one's abiding relationship with God must always take center stage. Second, all other relationships are fed by that intimate abiding relationship with God.

Imagine for a moment that you, along with every church leader and every member of your congregation, were totally focused on becoming like Jesus. How would that impact the relationships around you? Communication is one of the first things that comes to mind. What about listening? Dealing with difficult people? Getting past hurts? Forgiving? Showing unconditional love? Encouraging others? Handling conflict?

John D. Rockefeller once said, "I will pay more for the ability to deal with people than any other ability under the sun."[15] Rockefeller makes a good point: relationships are tough. Healthy relationships require a blend of honesty, selflessness, the strength to confront, the tenderness to console, the willingness to be flexible. The list goes on and on, and the requirements are not for the faint-hearted. That's why it is so important that God is empowering believers to make relationships work.

Jesus knew that without deep, heart-to-heart relationships life is meaningless. He concentrated on relationships. Jesus concentrated first on His relationship with His Father. The Scriptures repeatedly state that Jesus withdrew from all others to be with His Father. Jesus daily committed Himself to His relationship with His Father (Mark 1:35; Luke 5:16; Luke 6:12). Because of that empowerment, Jesus was then able to empower His relationships with His disciples and His relationships with every person He met. It stands to reason that when we believers follow the example of Jesus, our relationships take on new life.

Jesus touched the hearts of people with the love of God because the love of His Father flowed so strongly through Him. People longed to be near Jesus. The tenderness and caring that flowed from Jesus came from the Creator—and people wanted that life-giving Source to be part of their own lives. Isn't that what people are longing for today? Yes it is.

Leonard Sweet, says the Postmodernist is hungry for relationships.[16] Research backs him up. Recent studies indicate that just as many believers have experienced divorce as unbelievers. Is your church part of this divorce trend? What does this say about your church's current effectiveness in seeing relationships transformed? Obviously the majority of churches have missed the boat.

There is a way to turn these trends around however. It is by taking our focus off the latest trends in relational psychology and instead focusing on Christ-centered transformational discipleship. When we become like Jesus we are empowered to make other relationships work—and suddenly, miraculously—other people begin to want to become like Jesus. They want to cross the Bridge that spans the great divide between God and man. They want that same foundational relationship that so preoccupies the believer and that so evidently holds up the believer's life. They want to follow that grounded leader to God.

GET THIS ⇨ *The heart of this chapter…*
The core of spiritual transformation is a deep, abiding relationship with Jesus Christ. If we totally focus on becoming like Jesus, we will not grow weary in serving God. Instead we will continually glorify God in all our relationships.

GET PERSONAL ⇨ *How this applies to you and your church…*
Since you can never lead anyone beyond where you are yourself, you must let nothing interfere with your own personal relationship with Jesus. How is your personal relationship with Jesus closer today than it was this time last year? List things in your life that may be barriers to a closer relationship with Jesus. How can you demonstrate obedience in these specific areas that are blocking a closer relationship with Jesus? How does your relationship with Christ influence the relationships you have with others?

What opportunities does your church create to help its members form loving relationships with one another?

What opportunities does your church create to build relationships or impact the home church, work, school, and society?

On pages 25-33 we talked about character-based versus activity-based discipleship. Is your discipleship ministry more activity-based or character-based? Place a check mark along the spectrum of where you believe your church to be. Place an X along the spectrum of where you would like your church to be.

Activity-based   Character-based
←——————————————————————————————————————→

Since our activity-based Christian culture is so strong, what safeguards does your church take to ensure that the proper order of relationships are maintained by members of the church body? (1. God first. 2. Marriage second. 3. Children third. 4. Ministry fourth.)

What can you do as a church leader to constantly reinforce the importance of this relational order? How does a clear Jesus-focus help keep things in the proper order?

What changes can you make to the current support groups in your church during the next six months to make them more focused on Jesus in finding solutions to real-life problems?

GET GOING ⇨ *Tips for proactive discipleship…*
1. Ask people to pray and fast as they meditate on a Christ-centered life (spiritual transformation) and its critical role in relationships. Seek to lead people to know God's will for their church. Challenge every leader in various ministries to focus on building and growing their relationships continually and ask them to share.

2. Look for testimonies that can be shared on spiritually transformed lives from people who are growing in their walk and who are bearing fruit in love, joy, friendship, and service.

3. Regularly challenge people to realize the actions they take everyday

should have a foundation in the relationship they have with Christ.

4. Evaluate staff meetings, deacon meetings, teacher training, worship, preaching, prayer meetings, visitation, hospital calls in light of the relationship principle. Does every activity invite people to abide in Jesus and to know Him by Heart? If not, what might be changed?

5. Ask people to identify how church would be different if the relationship to Jesus was the most important aspect of church life and the people in the community.

6. Challenge every leader in various ministries to focus on building and growing their relationship continually and ask them to share.

7. Look for testimonies that can be shared on transformed lives from people who are growing in their walk and who are bearing fruit in love, joy, friendship, and service.

8. Encourage those you lead to team up with spiritual mentors and complete the study *The Mind of Christ* by T.W. Hunt to better understand how Jesus handled various relational issues: dealing with difficult people, getting past hurts, forgiving, showing unconditional love, handling conflict, encouraging one another.

[14] From sermon of Reverend Pat Hood, First Baptist Church Smyrna, Smyrna, Tennessee. Used by permission.
[15] John D. Rockefeller, *The Concise Columbia Dictionary of Quotations*, Robert Andrews, Ed. (New York: Columbia University press, 1987) M.
[16] Leonard Sweet, *A Cup of Coffee at the Soul Cafe*. (Nashville: Broadman & Holman Pub. © 1998) 28-29. All rights reserved.

I WILL FOLLOW HIM

Abiding in and following Jesus, glorifies God.

The Followship Principle:
Jesus calls every believer to follow Him.

The key to the followship principle rests in two profound words, *"I AM."* You see, the followship principle turns on a pivotal question every believer must answer: Is God sovereign? In other words, do you believe He has unlimited rule of and control over His creation? Is He sovereign to you? Is He sovereign to the believers in your church?

If He is—and we believe the Bible proves over and over that He is—then why are so many of us treading water? Why are we so reticent to follow the lead of Jesus and jump into the spiritual deep end with both feet? Why do we, instead, wade in and merely splash around in Christianity? What's keeping us from immersing ourselves in transformational discipleship and following Him? Two thousand years ago Jesus spoke two words that changed the course of history, *"Follow me"* (Matt. 4:19).

Today His message is the same. Jesus calls every believer to follow Him, but we resist being led by Jesus. We're gripping the side of the spiritual pool so tightly our knuckles are white. Disobedience is our sin nature at its worst, and it is draining the life out of our spiritual growth and our witness. No wonder most Christians are still in the wading pool of their spiritual journey. We're afraid to let go and let God make us everything we are supposed to be. Are we also afraid to truly life-guard those God has placed under our care by blowing the whistle and screaming, "Everybody into the deep end now!"—when we're not there ourselves?

What did Jesus really mean when He said those two words, *"Follow me"*? What are their implications for the church today and for us as church leaders?

Letting go and following Jesus into the spiritual deep end is the only way to glorify God. It's the only way to make a difference in this world. Jesus said in John 15:5 *"I am the vine; you are the branches. If a man remains in me and I in him, he will bear much fruit; apart from me you can do nothing."* Think about those words, *"Apart from me you can do nothing."* If we as believers merely wade around in Christianity, if we attempt to splash around with activities, programs, methods, and techniques but don't jump in the deep end and truly give our all to following Christ, to becoming like Him, we're dead in the water—and so is our witness.

The bottom line? We're terrified of letting go and going deep with God because we don't know God well enough to trust Him. So we don't obey Him.

Of course, following requires risk: • Does the leader know where he is going? • Does the leader have the follower's best interest at heart? •Is the leader trustworthy?

That's what is so perplexing about the average believer's refusal to wholeheartedly follow Jesus. He is the only leader throughout history who has never let a follower down. He's never lied. He's never misled. He's never made a selfish decision that His followers had to pay for. Jesus was a servant leader that proved over and over again with His life —and supremely with His sacrificial death—that He is completely trustworthy. Yet, amazingly, we still keep Him at arm's length.

God must sadly mourn the fact that so many of His children keep their distance. That so many of us love Him from the shallow end of the spiritual pool, when He wants us to know Him so He can reveal more fully His nature and perfect love. It's our distance that keeps us simply treading water. The fact is, the more we know God, the more we trust Him, and the more we trust Him, the more we obey Him. Then God brings us to a point where what He says to us will settle any issue forever. That's why Paul says, *Grow in the grace and knowledge of Him* (2 Pet. 3:18). But Paul also says combine that with love, *I pray also that the eyes of your heart may be enlightened in order that you may know the hope to which he has called you* (Eph. 1:18).

Experiencing "I AM"

Opening the eyes of our hearts to follow Jesus and leading others to follow Him is the path to experiencing the sovereignty of God. All the way through the Bible, "I AM" follows an experience. When Isaac was offered up for a sacrifice and "I AM" provided a substitute in the form of a ram caught in a thicket, Abraham experienced God in a way only someone who has jumped in the deep end of the pool can.

Abraham and many others in the Bible have had experiences that reveal "I AM" is totally trustworthy. They learned "I AM" will always provide, and that "I AM" is totally worthy of followship. So we should let nothing get in our way of following Him.

God wants total allegiance from His children. He wants His people to follow Him no matter what, for it is through such following that God shapes each believer to know Him in a little different way. He helped

Joseph to know a dimension of himself that could never have developed except through the circuitous route that God took him—from the depths of prison being faithful in tough circumstances to being highly exalted as second in command of a nation. God helped Paul become all he could be by blinding him on the road to Damascus and locking him up inside the prison walls of Rome. God also shaped David, the disciples, and Mary to know Him in a unique way. And He will shape and develop each of us if we will jump into the deep end as each of these believers did. God will shape us to match the requirements of the assignment He has for each of us. He will make us like Jesus.

Remember Who's Boss
Here's a sticking point. It is crucial that as deep-end believers we always remember that we are following; God is leading. Even in the deep end we don't win a community or nation for Him. We, instead, become the kind of people through whom God can bring a community or nation to Himself. The distinction is critical, for the second we begin to think it's us doing the doing, we'll sink to the bottom. We must remember that apart from Him we can do nothing, but with Him God can do anything through us. (See John 15:5.)

GET THIS ⇨ *The heart of this chapter…*
With the words *"Follow Me,"* Jesus carved a path to God for His disciples. He wants believers to follow Him no matter what, for it is through such faithful following that God shapes each believer to know Him in a unique way. He will reward each step of followship and will shape each believer to match the requirements of their special assignment. The result will be a life that glorifies God—just as the life of Jesus did.

GET PERSONAL ⇨ *How this applies to you and your church…*
Are there any areas in your life where you are being disobedient to God? An area you are holding back from Him? Explain why you believe you have failed to trust God with this area of your life. Given God's proven trustworthy character will you now surrender that area of your life that you have been holding back from Him?

Describe a time when God proved to you in a personal way that He is totally trustworthy and will always provide when you follow Him.

What steps can you take during the next six months to model follow-ship to others in your church?

What percentage of your church family believes they have a calling and are being obedient in carrying that out?

How can you demonstrate to your church body that God will shape us to match the requirements of the personal assignment He has for each of us? How will such a perspective empower your discipleship ministry?

GET GOING ⇨ *Tips for proactive discipleship...*

1. As a leader in your church, it is your responsibility to help provide a spiritually-sensitive environment that encourages believers to respond to Jesus' call to follow, one that challenges them to fulfill that call in the body of Christ, and one that develops their skills for service. One of the best first steps you can take is to close the distance between yourself and the believers in your church. Let them see you as a fellow follower not an exalted "power" with a spiritual life that stands hands above the average man. If you have kept your distance from those entrusted to your care or have exalted yourself as their leader, drop down on your knees and ask God's forgiveness and the forgiveness of those you have been entrusted to lead. Commit to begin sharing your own personal struggles, tragedies, and triumphs with individuals—not just the masses. Face-to-face, one-to-one relationship building was the style Jesus used for effective discipling. Granted, as a church leader you cannot cultivate a one-to-one relationship with everyone under your leadership, but by emulating the style of Jesus you teach others to emulate it. That's personalized discipleship-building that grows disciples.

2. If you have not already done so, begin a "Paul, Timothy, and Me" mentoring club in your church. Recruit older, more mature Christians to disciple younger ones, just as Paul discipled Timothy. After an established time of growth, encourage the younger Christian to then begin discipling an even younger Christian, such as a teenager or older child. This club will not only grow disciples in your church, it will grow leaders.

3. Ask your church leaders who they are following. How many people list the pastor, a staff member, a family member or friend. Who or how many identify Jesus as the leader? Discuss the difference between fol-

lowing God and following different leaders in the church. Identify how a church would be different if everyone sought to follow Jesus. How would the following be different? Worship? Sunday School? Every aspect of church?

4. Use this followship idea to study the Bible related to how believers deal with conflict when two followers disagree. Look for biblical examples when followers separated or united in their efforts to follow Christ.

5. Contrast followship with the story of the Pied Piper. How is this different?

6. Today a CEO model of pastoral leadership has emerged. How does followship challenge you as leader to be a following pilgrim? Will your congregation let the pastor use this model? How would your pastor or staff describe followship versus what the congregation followship is to be?

7. Study every biblical passage using "follow." Identify every public or private way your church has invited people to follow Christ. Is that done only in invitations? When and where else? Examine all the activities your church does. What percent call people to follow Him?

8. What would your church do differently if everyone saw themselves as seeking to follow Him? If every person in your church or community follow Jesus, where would that lead them?

9. Where is your church going? How many people connect their personal ministries with followship? How many of your church committees, teachers, deacons would say they are serving where they are out of a sense of call to follow Him?

10. Lead weekly prayer walks into every room in the church. Ask individuals to pray that the people who enter the sanctuary, classrooms, fellowship hall, offices, parking lots, and every other room in the church will come to know, love, trust, and obey God as Jesus did.

YOU'VE GOT THE POWER

The Empowerment Principle:
Believers must be empowered to serve.

When we abide in Jesus, He empowers us to make other relationships work.

NASA invests an enormous amount of time, money, and energy equipping and training the astronauts for success. The astronauts are guided throughout their mission by the unseen hands of NASA's engineering experts on earth. These "unseen hands" combined with well-trained astronauts—entrusted with great responsibility and the authority to take action—creates an empowered shuttle crew fully capable of successfully completing their intended mission.

Likewise, believers must be empowered to complete the greatest of all missions: taking the gospel to all people and making disciples. Throughout His three and a half-year ministry, Jesus empowered, equipped, discipled, trained, built-up, developed, and prepared His disciples to go and make disciples.

While on earth Jesus empowered His followers with His daily presence. But when He returned to His Father in heaven, He did not abandon those who needed His unceasing guidance. He continued to empower His disciples—not with His physical presence—but with His spiritual presence, the Holy Spirit. *"You will receive power when the Holy Spirit comes on you; and you will be my witnesses in Jerusalem, and in all Judea and Samaria and to the ends of the earth"* (Acts 1:8).

The Holy Spirit, the indwelling of Jesus in a disciple of Christ, empowered the first disciples and continues to empower each follower of Jesus Christ today. That means Jesus constantly abides with us, supplying never-ending power, perspective, and direction for our clearly stated common mission: to make disciples—to the ends of the earth.

Jesus Models Empowerment

Let's look closely at how Jesus empowered His disciples as we seek to disciple servant leaders in our churches who depend on His power.

In his book *Jesus on Leadership, Discovering the Secrets of Servant Leadership from the Life of Christ*, Gene Wilkes describes the empowering leadership of Jesus. Wilkes demonstrates how Jesus made sure His disciples understood both the responsibility and the authority He was sharing with them:

Jesus shared with His disciples the responsibility of bringing God's love to all peoples. That responsibility became their mission. It was huge! Eleven men to make disciples of all ethnic groups?! How was that possible? How did Jesus, as the leader of this eternal mission, empower his team of eleven to carry out this audacious goal…? First, Jesus had already accepted the responsibility…to reach all people with the love of God. His teachings and actions throughout his life showed his obedience to his heavenly Father's will. When Jesus called the disciples to himself on the side of a hill and commissioned them to continue that mission, he was not abdicating his own responsibility for it—he was sharing that responsibility. Servant leaders remain responsible for the mission even when they recruit others to complete it.

Jesus, however, did not share only his responsibility; he also shared his authority. *Responsibility without authority disables rather than empowers followers.* If you say, "Please help by doing thus and so, but don't make any decisions without checking with me," you have not empowered the person; you have enslaved him. Kennon Callahan reminds us that there must be a balance between delegated authority and responsibility. "More authority and fewer responsibilities help persons grow forward in their leadership; less authority and more responsibilities help persons develop passive behavior."[17]

Jesus remained steward of his Father's mission, but he enabled others to carry it out by sharing his authority with them. He did this when he said to his disciples of every generation: *"All authority in heaven and on earth has been given to me. Therefore go and make disciples"* (Matt. 28:18-19).[18]

Jesus guided His disciples from the perspective that every believer is a powerful minister. He shared His responsibility and His authority with them. The disciples learned they could serve and accomplish miracles in Jesus' name because of their relationship with Him. They were able to do more of the things Jesus did because He shared with them the responsibility and the authority to do those things. That's empowerment.

Is your church allowing empowered believers to serve? The church must nurture an environment of empowerment based on the truth that the Holy Spirit is the abiding presence that empowers the church to develop servant leaders who depend on His power. The Empowerment Principle blends perfectly with God's design of the body of Christ. Ephesians 1:22-23 makes it clear that the church exists because of Jesus Christ. And Romans 12:4-6a says, *Just as each of us has one body with many members, and these members do not all have the same function, so in Christ we who are many form one body, and each member belongs to all the others. We have different gifts, according to the grace given us.*

This passage is communicating, in part, that in a Christ-centered environment believers use their spiritual gifts to empower others in their own journeys to become more like Jesus. For example, those who don't have the gift of mercy are still called to be merciful—and who best can teach and train them than the one with that gift.

Ephesians 4:11-16 illustrates the spreading impact of empowerment. *It was he who gave some to be apostles, some to be prophets, some to be evangelists, and some to be pastors and teachers, to prepare God's people for works of service, so that the body of Christ may be built up until we all reach unity in the faith and in the knowledge of the Son of God and become mature, attaining to the whole measure of the fullness of Christ.*

Then we will no longer be infants, tossed back and forth by the waves, and blown here and there by every wind of teaching and by the cunning and craftiness of men in their deceitful scheming. Instead, speaking the truth in love, we will in all things grow up into him who is the Head, that is, Christ. From him the whole body, joined and held together by every supporting ligament, grows and builds itself up in love, as each part does its work.

The core strength of this passage is found in verses 15 and 16: *We will in all things grow up into him who is the Head, that is, Christ. From Him the whole body…grows and builds itself up….*

Once again we see Jesus as the primary relationship of every believer, the core of the church, the primary focus, the source of empowerment. And all other relationships must emanate from that core relationship with Him to be successful. Thus the success of your church's discipleship ministry must emanate from a core focus of becoming like Jesus. It must be empowered by Him.

Spreading Impact of Empowerment

As church leaders we are in the position to empower others to do the ministry of the church and carry out the Great Commission. Just as the character of Christ shaped and empowered His first disciples, the character of Christ empowers those we seek to shepherd.

As Jesus lived on earth, He modeled the important characteristics of honesty, vision, competence, and inspiration for His followers. Just as Christ modeled these characteristics of authentic relationships, we as church leaders must reflect and model them also if we are to encourage those in our churches to embrace Christ's desire that we make disciples.

One word of caution. Don't be surprised if everyone doesn't understand the purpose of a discipleship vision for your church. In Acts 16:10, we see Paul had a vision to go to Macedonia. This was after several failed attempts to go other places (Acts 16:6-8). *After Paul had seen the vision, we got ready at once to leave for Macedonia.* Paul was able to share his vision in such a way that others responded to the presence and working of the Holy Spirit. That's what you as a church leader must do if you are to shepherd your church's transformational discipleship ministry. You must share your vision and allow the Holy Spirit to work in hearts and create the momentum.

On-the-Job Training

Throughout Scripture Jesus chose ordinary people and entrusted ministry responsibilities to them, and then developed their character as they went along. When you look at Scripture, you'll notice some not-so-pretty character traits in the lives of the disciples. Such as James and John who wanted to sit next to Jesus, or Peter who was impulsive and headstrong. Yet, these were the very men to which the Savior entrusted His ministry. That says a lot about the huge investment of time and energy Jesus was willing to make in training and equipping these disciples on the job. If Jesus believed in empowering ordinary people, shouldn't we recognize His pattern when He does the same with those in our church?

The Follow-Me Empowerment System

Jesus' method of training was right out of His lifestyle and directly tied to His command to *"Follow me and I will make you fishers of men"* (Mark 1:17). Jesus clearly explained His vision for the disciples in advance. Then He set about empowering them to reach that vision through a five-point discipleship training model whose simplicity confused the scholars and whose effectiveness changed the world. It goes like this:

1. I do, you watch.
2. I do, you help (limited participation).
3. You do, I help.

4. You do, I watch.
5. You do, someone else watches.

The apostle Paul provides a great study of a disciple of Christ who effectively emulated this five-point training method for empowering other disciples. Acts 18 tells the story of Aquila and Priscilla, tentmakers Paul met in Corinth, who came to share Paul's goal to tell all people about Christ. The Gospel of Luke tells us that Paul *stayed and worked* (v. 3) with Aquila and Pricilla, effectively stepping through the first two stages of discipleship training. The two then traveled with Paul when he left Corinth and continued his missionary work in other areas. All along the way the Scriptures lead us to believe that Paul spent an enormous amount of time with these two believers, training them to do God's work. Empowering them to do it.

Eventually, Paul sensed these two were ready to help lead others. So he left them to grow the church in Ephesus, confident that he had prepared and trained them to do the ministry they had been called to do—and do it well. He empowered them to empower others.

In his book *Jesus on Leadership, Becoming a Servant Leader*, Gene Wilkes stresses that to follow Paul's pattern of training, you must…

1. Teach and model the gospel as you live and work with other believers.
2. Invite others to join you on your ministry team when you see they can contribute to the goal of your mission.
3. Allow them to take on ministry by themselves and form their own ministry teams.

Wilkes goes on to say, "If team members are not empowered, the leader does all the work."[19]

Ouch! Are you and a few others doing all the work in your church? It shouldn't be that way. Jesus modeled for every believer how to be empowered to lead others to the heart of God. Every believer is called to follow. Every believer is called to make disciples. Spiritual transformation demonstrated by making disciples is God's norm for believers, not the exception. God expects all believers to become like Jesus—and all have the opportunity to do so.

As a leader in your church it is your responsibility to see that others in your church are equipped to make disciples. It's the only way a discipleship ministry can reproduce and multiply. Obedience to the Great

Commission is the entry point of leadership development and training. Will you be obedient, let go the rigid hold of the reigns and seek daily to equip, train, and allow others to take those reigns? Will you encourage them to become like Jesus and lead others to the heart of God? Jesus calls you to obedience. Follow His lead. Make disciples who, in turn, make even more disciples. It's a multiplication effect that fulfills the command of the One who is still the steward of His Father's mission but who empowers His disciples with shared responsibility and authority, *"You will be my witnesses...to the ends of the earth"* (Acts 1:8).

GET THIS ⇨ *The heart of this chapter...*

Jesus guided His disciples from the perspective that every believer is a powerful minister. Throughout His three- and a half-year ministry on earth, Jesus prepared His disciples to fulfill the Great Commission. He did so with His personal presence. He shared His responsibility to bring God's love to all people and He shared His authority to do so. Today, through the indwelling of the Holy Spirit, Jesus continues to empower believers by sharing His responsibility and His authority. Church leaders are called to give responsibility and authority to believers to make disciples. It's the multiplication formula of Jesus Himself.

GET PERSONAL ⇨ *How this applies to you and your church...*

Leadership will make or break your discipleship ministry. If every believer is to develop a ministry, what steps does your church currently take to identify, recruit, and develop people to become leaders (not just workers and teachers, but all believers)?

How can you reorder your schedule to focus on discipleship-making and leadership development?

If you believe your church is part of God's work to spiritually transform lives, how would you say your church has helped you to live your faith at church, work, home, school, and in society? How would others answer the question if they were honest with you?

What steps can you take during the next year to begin implementing the empowerment system Jesus used?
1. I do, you watch.
2. I do, you help (limited participation).

3. You do, I help.
4. You do, I watch.
5. You do, someone else watches.

List 2–3 people you work with who you believe are at each of the five places in the training system, who's ready to go to the next step?

What steps can you take to give both responsibility and authority to others in your church to make disciples?

How can the development of small groups result in a multiplication of both leaders and disciples?

GET GOING ⇨ *Tips for proactive discipleship...*
1. Develop a transformational discipleship vision statement and a comprehensive plan for growing leaders in your church.

2. Complete the workbook study, *Jesus on Leadership, Becoming a Servant Leader* by Gene Wilkes with other leaders in your church to jump-start your leadership development program.

3. Page 68 discussed some character traits of ordinary people. What are the character traits in your church that might keep your church from developing transformational discipleship?

4. Review your attendance roles thinking in terms of who would say they feel equipped in a ministry (not just a church job). Pray that God would lead you to 8–12 people who would understand this empowerment through the Holy Spirit and would be willing to develop leaders by giving away their ministry and equipping others to serve.

5. A lot of this chapter speaks about giving responsibility and authority away to others. How many of your churches key leaders, including yourself, have a hard time giving ministry away? On a scale of 1–10, how big of an issue is control? Would you and other believers in your church be willing to give up leadership if it was better for the kingdom?

6. The way you respond to these last two ideas will determine how long it will take to develop a spiritual transformation concept and lead your

church to transformational discipleship.

7. Many churches have built programs to carry out the function of the church. How have these programs helped transform individuals and cultures? Hindered? How might your ministry be different?

8. Ask a group of your leaders how Christ empowers them. Use their responses to challenge them to identify and model Christ's presence in their lives.

[17] Kennon L. Callahan, *Effective Church Leadership* (New York: Harper and Row, 1990), 157.
[18] C. Gene Wilkes, *Jesus On Leadership: Discovering the Secrets of Servant Leadership from the Life of Christ* (Nashville: LifeWay Press, 1998) 180-182.
[19] C. Gene Wilkes, *Jesus On Leadership, Becoming a Servant Leader* (Nashville: LifeWay Press, 1996) 109,112.

THIS IS YOUR LIFE

The Lifestyle Principle:
Transformed believers naturally express biblical examples and insights in everyday life.

A young soldier, who grew up in a fisherman's family on the banks of Lake Pontchartrain, speaks of his father's hard life.

"My father was a Christian man. No matter how hard making a living fishing was, he never failed to give God credit for anything good, and he had ultimate faith that God was going to see us through when things were bad. I didn't pay much attention to his attempts to lead me to faith in Jesus when I was growing up. But after Papa died, I attended church and listened to the preacher describe Jesus and tell about His life. I was amazed and moved. I realized I'd already known a man like that—my Papa."[20]

To know "Papa" was to know Jesus. Through God's transformational power the hardworking fisherman became like Jesus—and by doing so he touched the heart of his own son. God pulled others toward Himself through this simple fisherman's everyday life. His intimate relationship with Jesus bore witness of Jesus' love. When this man's children, spouse, friends—and even total strangers—came in contact with him, they were in the presence of Jesus. They were drawn to Jesus through the fisherman's everyday witness. His life—and the stories he told about it—spoke volumes about Who lived in his heart.

When Jesus begins living out His life through a transformed believer, it changes everything and everyone that believer meets. God uses transformed hearts to forever change children, spouses, friends—even strangers on the street. Just as He used the old fisherman, God will use you and the other believers in your church to point the way to Himself—if you choose to give your hearts to the transformed life.

Transformed believers naturally honor God's name by expressing biblical examples and insights in everyday living. There is no separation of "church and state" for the transformed believer; all things are viewed through the lens of Scripture and all actions are measured by the tape: "How will this affect my relationship with Jesus?"

Lifestyle becomes a daily opportunity to bear witness that we are the children of God. *"It's who you are and the way you live that count before God"* (1 John 4:23, *The MESSAGE*).

The bulk of Scripture is story after story of diverse, ordinary, common people who honored God's name with their lifestyles. Aquila and Priscilla were tentmakers by trade and God's witnesses by heart. Even while making tents they comfortably expressed to their friends, their family members, and even strangers what God was doing in their lives. (They probably had lots of interesting stories to tell about traveling with a strong personality like Paul!)

Aquila and Priscilla wove the fabric of Jesus into the lives of everyone they met. Disciple-making was their real career, not tent-making. They lived their internal spiritual transformation out loud.

Every believer, regardless of age or length of time as a Christian, is a unique treasure from God with a story to share. One role of the church is to encourage its believers to step out and comfortably share their spiritual stories with family, friends, acquaintances, and strangers. The best way to accomplish such sharing is in our day-in and day-out conversations and events. Extravagant communication is rarely as effective an intimate conversation. What may seem like a small story to one, can open the sealed heart of another. It is in the *everyday, ordinary life—your sleeping, eating, going-to-work, and walking-around life* (Rom. 12:1, *The MESSAGE*) that believers experience God. And it is by sharing these everyday experiences that believers help others experience God too.

The grandfather who tells his grandson about God's creation while walking through the woods is using a simple moment of life to make a disciple. The mother who tucks her daughter into bed at night with a story about how God protected her from danger when she was a child, is making a disciple. The friend who stands by another friend during a crisis and shares encouraging words and Bible verses is making a disciple. The old fisherman who praised God whether the nets were full or empty was making a disciple of his son. These simple, ordinary, life-moments impact the world for Jesus and glorify God. They are not grand gestures for show; but the natural expression of Jesus living out His life in ordinary people. They are ordinary events with extraordinary impact.

Sharing one's testimony for Christ should not be confined to five-minute speeches in front of a congregation of people. In the life of the spiritually transformed believer, testimony is a constant communication that speaks through the life the believer lives and the stories he shares every day. For the transformed believer, the Christian lifestyle is not a strain; it is an honor.

These commandments that I give you today are to be upon your hearts.

Impress them on your children. Talk about them when you sit at home and when you walk along the road, when you lie down and when you get up (Deut. 6:6-7).

GET THIS ⇨ *The heart of this chapter…*

Transformed believers naturally honor God's name by expressing biblical examples and insights in everyday living. There is no separation of "church and state" for the transformed believer; all things are viewed through the lens of Scripture and all actions are measured by the tape: "How will this affect my relationship with Jesus?" Lifestyle is a daily opportunity to bear witness that we are the children of God.

GET PERSONAL ⇨ *How this applies to you and your church…*

Who has been a spiritual role model for your ministry? How does this person's lifestyle reflect his or her relationship with Jesus? How has this person communicated the story of his/her faith walk with you and others?

Think of five people you can share your own faith walk story with this month. Encourage those involved in small groups in your church to also share their faith walk stories with five people this month. Such sharing will not only help those who share to see the evidences of transformation in their lives, but it will also be a witness of God's power to others.

GET GOING ⇨ *Tips for proactive discipleship…*

1. Every believer, regardless of age or length of time as a Christian, is a unique treasure from God with a story to share, a unique discipleship tool. Thus, one role of the church is to encourage its believers to step out and comfortably share what God has done with family, friends, acquaintances, and strangers.

2. One way to encourage such sharing is to incorporate small groups into your church structure. Train group leaders to set aside time at each small-group meeting for members to share personal stories of God's work in their lives.

3. Challenge each group to keep a testimony book in which members take turns recording their stories on paper. Several times a year have each group leader choose stories from their book to share in a special

service with other small groups. Leaders should encourage members to share their stories with those outside their small groups.

4. As a church body, memorize Deuteronomy 6:6-7 as a guiding light for sharing personal stories of faith and hope with others.

5. Ask all Sunday School teachers to encourage their students to share personal stories in class. This is an especially effective discipleship tool for children and teens. Teachers can also encourage journaling as a personal record of God's work in each believer's life.

6. Pass out note cards to everyone at a worship or prayer service. Ask them to write a note of affirmation to a person who lives their faith everyday. Ask them to deliver or mail their note sometime during the week.

7. Ask the congregation to share favorite biblical examples of individuals who lived their faith in their everyday life and tell how that has encouraged them.

8. Over a period of weeks interview significant people who have modeled their faith in the community.

9. Interview people who would share testimonies of others who have shared biblical examples or demonstrated their faith in their lifestyle.

10. Ask a father and/or mother to share what they hope their church teachers will teach their children.

11. Review the common occurrences in a person's life (birth, school, job, promotion, downsizing, marriage, children leaving home, death, etc.). Ask a group of key leaders to pray about how their church can minister to these individuals and families through these passages.

[20] As told by Ralph Hodge, LifeWay Christian Resources, Nashville, Tennessee.

HONOR THE NAME

The Accountability Principle:
Every believer is accountable to God.

There is an old story of a rebellious, undisciplined soldier brought before the commander of his division for discipline. As the young man stood on trembling knees, the leader asked him his name. When he answered, the leader burst into full fury at the young soldier.

"Son! That's my last name too, and because my name is the same as yours, your actions bring dishonor to me! So you have two choices—either change your name or change your life!"

This young soldier learned an important lesson. When you bear someone's name whatever you do brings either honor or shame to that name. As believers we bear the name of Jesus; therefore, it is vital that we honor His name with our everyday actions and attitudes. It is vital that we take seriously the charge to make disciples. For you see—we are accountable to God.

The measure of discipleship is the degree to which a believer is like Jesus in attitudes, behavior, and relationships. In Romans 14:12 the Bible says, *Each of us will give an account of himself to God.* So here we stand as children of God, sharing His name—and either bringing Him shame or glory. That's no small responsibility. It requires a commitment to love, trust, and obey as Jesus did.

Jesus' life brought honor and glory to God. Not once did Jesus shame His Father's name. We probably aren't even aware of all the times we bring dishonor to God. Oh, we may remember the big moments, the blatant instances. But there are so many things we choose to be blind to—sinful parasites that cling to our lives and bring shame to God's name. For instance, we shame God's name when we use it in a meaningless, casual way or when we are surprised or distraught. The third commandment says, *"You shall not misuse the name of the Lord your God, for the Lord will not hold anyone guiltless who misuses his name"* (Ex. 20:7). We are accountable to God when we use His holy name in a meaningless way. We are accountable to Him to utter it only in reverence, in respect, in worship, and in awe.

We also bring dishonor to God's name when we have temper

tantrums while standing in long lines at a store, when we express road rage, when we selfishly ignore someone in need, or when we make watching the Super Bowl more important than worshiping the Lord. Finally, we bring dishonor to God's name when we fail to obey God's primary charge to us as believers: make disciples. These dishonorable actions are not the ways of Jesus. They are the ways of sinful man. Jesus did not start yelling and screaming at the bread seller for only having one line open. Jesus did not run people off the road when they weren't traveling to fit His schedule. Jesus did not yell "Get a job!" to the homeless man on the street. Jesus did not skip His time with the Father to watch the Roman games. And Jesus certainly did not let anything deter Him from His mission of making disciples. Jesus obeyed His Father and thus brought honor and glory to His Father's name. We are called to do the same—and when we do not, God holds us accountable for each and every instance of disobedience.

One of the most important things a church must do is teach believers to obey everything Jesus commanded, to live and honor God's name as He did (Matt. 28:20). By teaching obedience, the church naturally teaches the accountability principle.

Although believers are accountable to God, God uses the church, spouse, other family members, friends, and fellow believers to keep one another aware of accountability to Him. In essence God has created natural accountability groups to help the believer focus on becoming like Jesus. These natural accountability groups help the believer put God first and honor His name—not out of fear of reprisal, but out of love and respect—just like Jesus did. *"'Love the Lord your God with all your heart and with all your soul and with all your strength and with all your mind'; and 'Love your neighbor as yourself'"* (Luke 10:27).

GET THIS ⇨ *The heart of this chapter…*
The measure of discipleship is the degree to which a believer is like Jesus in attitudes, behavior, and relationships. In Romans 14:12, the Bible says, *Each of us will give an account of himself to God.* As believers we bear the name of God; therefore, it is vital that we honor His name with our everyday actions and attitudes. It is vital that we take seriously the charge to make disciples. For you see—we are accountable to God for all we do—and all we do not do.

GET PERSONAL ⇨ *How this applies to you and your church...*

What accountability safeguards do you have around yourself as a church leader? Who do you ask to hold you accountable?

How does your church encourage members' accountability to honor God's name in everyday actions and attitudes and to make disciples as a natural part of everyday life?

GET GOING ⇨ *Tips for proactive discipleship...*

1. One of the most important things a church must do is teach believers to obey everything Jesus commanded, to live and honor God's name as He did. By teaching obedience, your church naturally teaches the accountability principle. How can you and other church leaders model obedience for the church body?

2. Although believers are accountable to God, God uses the church, spouse, other family members, friends, and fellow believers to keep one another aware of accountability to Him. In essence God has created natural accountability groups to help the believer focus on becoming like Jesus. Develop an accountability training module that teaches the believers in your church the biblical way to confront a believer who is bringing dishonor to the name of Jesus. Teach them that every believer's ultimate accountability is to God.

3. How would the believer in your church be different if church members sought to reflect Jesus in attitudes, behavior and relationships? Ask a group in your church (Sunday School teachers/classes, a discipleship group, deacons, the choir, the church staff, a committee or a transformational discipleship task force) to make three lists. One listing would include attitudes expressed among church members over a 1–2 week period of time. Another list would include behaviors observed among members. A third list would include all the characteristics found among relationships in the church. Compile the lists, then meet together to discuss and pray about your church's attitudes, behavior, and relationships.

4. Determine actions that could be taken to improve these three lists. Ask the group to think about how accountable is the church for these lists and what could be done about them to better reflect the Lord's glory.

5. The accountability principle calls for a church to be accountable and to call people to be accountable for their attitudes, actions/behavior, and relationships. This principle calls every church to help believers live their faith everyday in every sphere of influence it touches. How does your church teach accountability and responsibility to its members? How often has the church taken a stand based on the members' desire to be like Christ?

6. The world is moving in a direction contrary to biblical truth. Identify actions the church can take to help believers live for Christ in society and to make disciples.

7. A lot of the accountability principle focuses on trusting, loving, and, especially, obeying God. How does your church call people to obey Him? Study the hymn "Trust and Obey." Make it the theme of a series of messages. Help people see the connection between trusting, loving, and obeying. Identify how obedience relates to trusting and loving. Identify why people don't like to obey.

8. Review resources that can be studied by groups in your church to help members learn to trust, love, and obey Him. Use these materials to begin study groups.

9. Oftentimes pastors, teachers, and church members get into routines or ruts, or feel like they just go in circles. Invite speakers to your church to share with your congregation how God sometimes requires perseverance as well as openness to new assignments.

10. Ask your people to identify all the things that would have to change and all the things that would stay the same in your church if everyone realized that Jesus is your church's accountability partner.

11. Consider asking the pastor and a few church members of another church to serve as "accountability consultants" for your church, meeting with you regularly to listen about your church's obedience and to hold you accountable to God to help believers to be spiritually transformed by learning to trust, love, and obey God.

KNOW WHEN TO BEND

> **The Flexibility Principle:**
> Diverse people need flexible and adaptable ways to
> experience spiritual transformation.

A tornado swept through Nashville in 1998, causing downed trees and shredded power lines. In a scene of devastation, one old maple tree was still standing, proud and tall, though it had taken a wicked beating.

A few days later, while tree surgeons were removing other trees from roofs, yards, and the windows of parked cars, people wondered why the maple had withstood the storm while others toppled. When asked how the maple had survived the storm, the tree surgeon replied: "Well, two things were in its favor—one, it had been recently trimmed of dead branches and its healthy ones had been pruned. That made the tree stronger than the ones lying in the street. Two, just from looking at the way the tree grows, I can tell it has been able to bend over the years. When high winds come, knowing how to bend can make all the difference in the world."[21]

Knowing how to bend. Pruning healthy limbs. Cutting away dead limbs. The story of the maple tree emphasizes the need and value of flexibility. You see, the church is made up of diverse people of all learning styles, personality types, genders, ages, family types and situations, cultural backgrounds, economic conditions, and ethnic backgrounds. Such a melting pot needs flexible and adaptable ways for these diverse people to experience spiritual transformation.

The Flexible Church

The word *flexible* means to be "capable of change, to adapt to new, different circumstances, to adjust." Simply put, a flexible church is one that knows how and when to adjust.

The Gospels record various approaches Jesus used to disciple diverse people. He was always matching His discipling methods to best meet the unique personalities and special needs of those He discipled.

Jesus …

- used parables to get down on the everyday person's level. (Matt. 13:10-23)
- tailored an in-your-face mentoring approach for head-strong disciples like Peter. (John 13:6-17)

- gently guided a frightened woman to God—wrote softly in the sand, even while others raised stones. (John 8:3-11)
- took the time for conversations with James and John, daily challenging them to become more like the Father. (Mark 3:13-17)
- made Himself comfortably at home in small groups to draw people like Mary and Martha closer to Him. (John 12:2-8)
- invested considerable time in long-term, intimate, personal relationships with people like Lazarus. (John 11)
- joined others in worship on the Sabbath day in the synagogue, as was His custom. (Luke 4:16)
- taught His disciples that actions often speak louder than words when He threw the moneychangers out of the temple. (Matt. 21:12-13)
- often left the needy masses to pray in solitude. (Matt. 26:36)

What Jesus taught by example with His own discipleship style is this: *Spiritual transformation can take place in each unique individual who has a personal relationship with Jesus.* To disciple as Jesus did, your church must ensure that its structures, organizations, processes, and procedures facilitate the Holy Spirit's work of spiritual transformation in flexible and adaptable ways. This includes methods and messages appropriate for the different types of people God has creatively blended into your church.

Mechanical vs. Organic

In their book, *Growing Spiritual Redwoods*, Bill Easum and Thomas Bandy refer to two different kinds of church structures: mechanical and organic.[22] One operates or functions like a machine, while the other is a living, growing organism that flexes and adapts to a multitude of environmental factors. As we discussed in the first chapter of this resource, Jesus is in the business of changing selfish people into servant leaders. The church's role is to create a warm, nurturing environment that fosters this miraculous metamorphosis. It stands to reason then, that an organically-based church is far more likely to produce a warm, nurturing environment than a mechanical one.

But what does *organic* really mean? Do we toss out all our data bases, junk our organizational charts, say goodbye to scheduling and suddenly just start to "be" church? Absolutely not. Just as our physical bodies need an infrastructure to hold us together, the church body needs infrastructure to keep it in one piece. The programs, organizational systems, and established procedures carefully orchestrated by the Holy Spirit, through you and other church leaders make up the vital structure of a church.

The church structure should enable or support the other organs of the body; it should make it possible for the other parts to accomplish what they are designed to do. Anytime a structure becomes a hindrance to the parts of the body functioning according to their design, it is a malfunctioning structure. Take a look at your church. Is its structure impeding the God-given calling of becoming like Jesus?

The Bible says that new wine cannot be stored in old wineskins. (See Matt. 9:17.) The fresh movement of the Spirit in a church focused on becoming like Jesus will indeed burst old structures. Yet, we continue to fight hard to keep the old structures in place. When we witness this phenomenon in churches across the country it's a reminder of the old man in the movie *Fiddler on the Roof* who, in the opening moments of the movie, sings the praises of "tradition." But when asked the reason for tradition, he fumbles and stumbles and finally answers that he doesn't know. As church leaders, many of us hang on to the traditions and structures of our churches just because they have always been in place, not because they are working. If a discipleship ministry is to thrive in your church there must be enough flexibility to put responsiveness to the Spirit ahead of established tradition.

Once again let us emphasize that structures are necessary. Note that Jesus did not say, "Men do not pour new wine into NO wineskins." If we do not have some structures in place, we'll have chaos. The structures of today will be the very ones that will keep your church from growing in the future—if they do not remain responsive and pliable.

The key to a healthy church and a vibrant transformational discipleship mindset is: *The structure of a church must be adaptable to change.* Although great caution must be taken to never compromise the message of the gospel, there must be a willingness to mold and shape methodology. Just as our physical bodies get sick when organs do not function properly, so the body of Christ becomes vulnerable to disease when various parts are not properly nurtured.

A Foundation for Flexibility

We are doing a lot of flexing here, but we would be remiss if we did not state that there are some essential elements a flexible discipleship ministry needs as a strong base. This first is:

• A clear mission statement.

We are not talking about fancy words on paper that are filed away in a filing cabinet in the church office. We're talking about a living, breathing, regularly communicated mission statement that clearly explains what the discipleship ministry of your church is all about. This mission statement must be one that provides an internal compass for ensuring that your transformational discipleship ministry stays on a gospel-based track—even if it takes different paths to reach different people.

Let's look at a few mission statements that some churches are using to guide their transformational discipleship programs:

↪ Leading people to embrace Christ and glorify God through worship, evangelism, discipleship, fellowship, and service.

↪ Helping people trust, love, and obey God for His glory.

↪ Increasingly know Him and make Him known.

↪ Seeking to become like Jesus.

What makes these mission statements so effective is that they all set their sights on the goal of becoming like Jesus and helping others become like Him. This is the filter that keeps the focus on Jesus.

• Evaluation process.

Next in line is the built-in "evaluation process" for pruning the productive and weeding out things that distract from the core purpose.

The ongoing evaluation process is simply a regular time to evaluate the effectiveness of the discipleship infrastructure. Some of the questions to ask are:

1. Is the activity in accord with Scripture?
2. Is the activity supporting the purpose statement of the church and this specific ministry?
3. Is this activity helping to create a church-wide environment for spiritual transformation?
4. Are believers being reached, nurtured, and transformed?
5. Are believers being developed into leaders?
6. Is the structure reproducible?

These are simple questions that can keep your church constantly aware of progress—or the lack thereof—because a discipleship ministry that isn't beefing up is a ministry that has problems deep down.

Your church will determine what actions need to be taken to help create an environment for spiritual transformation during the evaluation process. Creating and maintaining functional structures is an ongoing process of evaluation. Evaluation is a process of removing, pruning, and cultivating. Ongoing training cultivates fruitfulness (on-the-job training and apprenticeship). Consistent evaluation reveals when additional resources may be needed (financial, curriculum, people power).

Using John 15 and the vine-dresser illustration regarding fruit—or the lack thereof—as the test for effective discipleship. An effective evaluation process will:

⇨ Help your church stop and pull the plug on some non-productive programs (remove from the vine);

⇨ Help your church focus efforts on those things that are producing so they will produce even more fruit (pruning);

⇨ Train your church to ask the right questions of how the effectiveness of what's working can be improved (shaping);

⇨ Help your church zero-in on areas where an increase in finances is needed and pinpoint where leaders need more empowerment (cultivate);

⇨ Enable your church to multiply the ministry (reproduction).

More Is Better

A reproducible structure enables the discipleship ministry to expand according to its purpose. This increases the capacity of ministry—more people becoming more like Jesus every day. What are some issues to consider in determining if your discipleship ministry is reproducible?

—Are new believers being nurtured and cultivated into the life of the church?

—Is the next generation of leaders being developed?

—Is Scripture being applied to issues that come up in the church?

The Potential of Groups

One discipleship method that seems to naturally incorporate all the principles we have discussed thus far is small groups. Perhaps that's why Christian Schwarz says, "If we were to identify any one principle as the 'most important,' then without a doubt it would be the multiplication of small groups. Small groups are the pillar of church growth."[23] The dynamics of small groups seem to emulate the dynamics Jesus cultivated when growing the faith of His own twelve disciples.

Let's look at the dynamics of small groups and how they can help facilitate a vibrant discipleship ministry in your church. The early church at Jerusalem gives some guidance for the necessary elements of healthy small groups. (See Acts 2:42-47.) Its dynamics include:

1. Power—the outpouring of the Holy Spirit;
2. Leadership—leaders giving wisdom and direction;
3. Prayer—listening to God, interceding in prayer for others and for the work of God.
4. Worship—praising God;
5. Teaching—learning and applying God's Word;
6. Fellowship—nurturing and building relationships;
7. Ministry—meeting the needs of others based on giftedness;
8. Evangelism—sharing the gospel, impacting society, people being added to the church (the body of Christ);
9. Accountability—holding one another accountable to God;
10. Encouragement—seeking to uplift one another's spiritual and emotional health;
11. Support—standing by one another in difficult and trying circumstances.

If you would like to add small groups to the flexible roster of discipleship methods in your church, there are several issues regarding small groups you will need to address. We offer a summation here to use as a reference tool for your development.

• *How Many People Should Be in Each Group?*

Small-group experts agree the ideal size group should be 3 to 15. Remember, Jesus Himself chose twelve to be a part of the small group He led. As the group gets larger than 10-12, group dynamics change. The larger the group, the easier it becomes for a quiet person to hide in a spiritual and emotional sense. The larger the group, the more difficult it becomes to nurture each person.

• *What Will Be the Makeup of the Membership?*

Will the group be made up of people that are all about the same age? What about education levels? Socioeconomic status? Men/women only, or couples? Most people like to be with others like themselves. Commonality promotes closer relationships and quicker group development.

• *Will the Group(s) Be Open or Closed Groups?*

Simply put, an open group is open to new members coming into the life of the group at any time. A closed group intentionally closes membership to new members at some point in the group's development; typically early in the development. Both types have strengths and weaknesses. Open groups allow for quicker assimilation of new people. Closed groups allow for more intimate relationships and higher accountability. To glean from the strengths of both types of groups you could consider doing a combination. The group may remain open for the first six weeks or so of the group's life then close the group for a period of time (maybe 12 months or so). Then open the group again for some to leave and new people to come in. Remember a permanently closed group will eventually stagnate as does any system that closes.

• *How Long Should a Group Remain a Group?*

Here again the options are numerous and they depend on your goals and situation. Groups can remain as a group from several weeks to a year or more. Naturally the longer a group meets the deeper the relationships get and the higher the accountability becomes. However, most people do not want to be a part of group that has unstated limits. At the end of the time decided upon, the group may dissolve and members become a part of other groups or the groups could form an additional group through an intentional multiplication process.

• *How Often Do the Groups Meet?*

Ideally groups would meet on a weekly basis. It is difficult to build the relationships and accountability desired if a group meets less frequently. But once again, there are options. Most small-group experts agree that less than every two weeks is not sufficient for impact on individual lives.

• *What Should the Schedule Be for Small Groups and Where Should They Meet?*

One of the strengths of small groups is their flexibility as to when and where they should meet. The simple answer here is wherever and whenever agreed upon by the group members. Transformational discipleship is a 24/7 ministry. Member homes make great locations for group meetings. An open group also creates another entry point into the life of the church as unchurched people are invited to be a part of the group.

• *What About Leadership for the Groups?*

Leadership is the key to a successful small-group ministry. Most churches that are successful with small groups have come to understand the strength of an apprentice process. Each group has at least one apprentice that is in training to lead a new group. This apprentice may be given some basic training to understand the philosophy of that particular church's small-group ministry as well as group dynamics. He or she is then given some leadership responsibilities by the leader of the group they are a part of. After beginning their own small group, all leaders take part in some type of ongoing on-the-job training.

• *What About the Children?*

Churches handle this challenge in a number of ways. The group may decide to rotate with different members taking turns watching the children in another room of the home in which they meet. The group members may pitch in and bring in someone from outside the group to watch the children in another room of the house in which they meet. Some groups might decide to trade off with other groups. Group 1 watches the children of Group 2 on Tuesdays and Group 2 watches the children of Group 1 on Thursdays. Again, the options are numerous.

• *What About Starting New Groups?*

Hopefully most of the groups that form see themselves expanding and starting new groups right from the start. An existing group starts a new group by sending out either the leader or the apprentice to begin the new group. Several of the members of the existing group could go with the leader or apprentice to allow room for new members in the old group. This keeps the system open and allows new members to be a part of the small groups, thus eliminating stagnation. New groups can also be started as new leaders are trained. The new leader would want to find an apprentice as soon as possible in the process.

Remaining Flexible

It would be impossible to describe the many ways you can incorporate flexibility into your discipleship ministry, because the choices are as diverse as the individuals that make up your church. We have described small groups in detail here, but other approaches may be the perfect match for many under your sphere of influence. The key is to match approach with what works best for different learning styles, personality types, genders, ages, family types and situations, cultural backgrounds, economic conditions, and ethnic backgrounds. Remaining flexible enables you and your church to cultivate a discipleship ministry that is uniquely personal and constantly focused on Christ.

Jeremiah 29:11 is a flagship Scripture that illustrates the personal attention God offers every believer. *"For I know the plans I have for you,"* *declares the Lord, "plans to prosper you and not to harm you, plans to give* *you hope and a future."*

Use the Flexibility Principle undergirded by this promise of God to help you bend, mold, shape, and adapt your discipleship ministry to fit God's plans to give hope and a future to all who belong to Him. Because, just as Jesus taught by example, *spiritual transformation is unique* *to each individual who has a personal relationship with Him.*

GET THIS ⇨ *The heart of this chapter...*
The church can be made up of diverse people of all learning styles, personality types, genders, ages, family types and situations, cultural backgrounds, economic conditions, and ethnic backgrounds. Such a melting pot needs flexible and adaptable ways for these diverse people to experience spiritual transformation. Forcing everyone into a rigid mold results in a discipleship ministry that can be easily uprooted.

GET PERSONAL ⇨ *How this applies to you and your church...*
How are current ministries meeting the diverse needs of the people in your church and in your community?

List the primary ways your church uses to make disciples. Then, on a scale of 1 to 10, with 1 being the least flexible and 10 being the most, rate your church's flexibility in incorporating a variety of discipling methods.

If you scored your church low, what steps can you take to help make your church more flexible as it seeks to disciple people of different perspectives and needs?

What other discipleship methods of Jesus could you begin developing that would reach other people in your church and community who want to grow in Christ? (See pp. 81-82 for a listing of discipling methods Jesus used.)

List the types of people whose discipleship needs you believe your church is effectively meeting.

Now, list those whom the church could respond to in ways that would match their discipleship needs.

What steps can you take as a church leader to begin adapting church programs to better match the needs of these groups of people?

GET GOING ⇨ *Tips for proactive discipleship...*
1. Spiritual transformation is unique to each individual who has a personal relationship with Jesus. To disciple as Jesus did, your church must ensure that its structures, organizations, processes, and procedures sup-

port the Holy Spirit's work of spiritual transformation in flexible and adaptable ways. This includes methods and messages appropriate for the different types of people God may have creatively blended into your church.

2. On pages 81-82, nine discipling methods of Jesus are identified (parables, in-your-face-mentoring, soft guidance, leisurely conversations, small groups, personal relationships, teaching disciples, and praying in solitude). Review these with your deacons. Ask them to identify methods of discipleship that they feel comfortable or uncomfortable with. Help them to take on the role of a disciple-maker—connecting their life with their faith.

3. Give this flexibility test to groups in your church.
Answer true or false.
   —It is a big deal in your church if the order of worship changes each week.
   —When the Sunday morning schedule is adjusted, people don't like it.
   —If the Sunday School classes are changed or divided people get upset.
   —Worship routine is more important than leading people to experience the presence of God.
   —How something is done is more important than the lives that are affected.
   Add other questions more relevant to your community. Use the questionnaire to lead your church to evaluate why it does what it does and to focus on its purpose. Help the church to see its role in developing believers to be spiritually transformed. Lead the church to distinguish between an organic and mechanical church (see pp. 82-83).

4. Draw an organizational chart of your church. Ask others to do the same. Compare different people's view of the organizations of your church. Notice differences and similarities. How has it changed over the years? How would people describe the purpose of their church? If the organizational charts you've drawn is the skeleton of your church, how does it support the body? How should it change? (See pp. 82-83.)

5. Page 84 identifies several mission statements. Share these with several groups in your church. Ask them to identify which ones seem to de-

scribe what your church is about. If these don't seem appropriate, have everyone write down ideas that seem to describe your mission. Distribute a list of activities your church has done in the last year. Discuss how these approaches could or should support your mission. Talk about ways your church can be on mission with God to make disciples and align its activities to that mission.

6. Create prayer teams to pray for your church and its mission.

7. How will you use the activities on pages 84-85 (the evaluation process and John 15) to lead your church to depend on God for spiritual transformation. Plan a time line to utilize these approaches to grow God's ministry in your church.

8. Make a list of all the groups in your church. Which ones are open or closed. How do they function? How dependent on the staff are they? What can they accomplish relative to your mission? What could be done for the kingdom if small groups were a major vehicle of your church? Use pages 85-88.

[21] Adapted from *Home Again* by Ivey Harrington. Used by permission.
[22] William M. Easum and Thomas G. Bandy, *Growing Spiritual Redwoods* (Nashville: Abingdon Press, 1997) 111-115.
[23] Christian A. Schwarz, *Natural Church Development, A Guide to Eight Essential Qualities of Healthy Churches*, © 1996 Christian A. Schwarz. 32-33.

A CHURCH THAT "GETS IT"

Helping every believer to understand how they are to abide in Christ is central to everything your church is and does.

On May 15, 1999, I (Barry) boarded a plane en route to a place called Mombasa, Kenya. How different Kenya was from my home. I saw more poverty in one hour, than I was accustomed to seeing in a year. Little did I know I was going to travel half-way around the world to land right in the middle of a place where God was so mightily at work.

My first preaching assignment was in a village called Kwali, located about an hour and a half from Mombasa. It was there that I had an encounter with a church that "got it"!

The church building itself, or what there was of it, was located about 500 yards behind a gas station and bar. Mud was everywhere since May in Kenya is right in the middle of the rainy season. The church building was four walls of homemade blocks with no doors, no windows, and no roof! (You entered through the openings between the walls.) The entire area inside the walls was mud.

My first thoughts as I stood in deep mud inside the wall area were, *Lord, Where have You brought me?* and *Will anybody show up?*

His answers were loud and clear. People started arriving from every direction. Soon I met the pastor and other leaders of the church. There was a footlocker in the corner of the structure that was covered with palm leaves. To my surprise, this is where the choir robes and offering plates were kept.

Soon the worship service started and I saw the kingdom of God reigning in the lives of those people evidenced by the presence of the Holy Spirit in and through them. Right there before my eyes, the church became manifest just as in the early church. Their fellowship and worship was engaging and sincere. God was their audience and I was convinced He was pleased. I preached using an interpreter for the first time. Never before had I seen people so focused on God's word and message.

As people were responding to God's call, my interpreter explained to me that two of the women responding were from a Muslim background. Now that they had received the gift of salvation many things in their lives would change. One thing was certain. These women knew they could not go back home. The church began making other accommodations for them.

Another woman had come to church seeking comfort and hope. Her father had died and his home was hundreds of miles away. The church took an extra offering to get her enough money for a bus ticket.

Another family's home had been destroyed and the men of the church were putting together a plan to build it back. Ministry was taking place all around me. These people were responding with love, trust, and obedience. They were glorifying God with their lives!

The overwhelming presence and evidence of the Holy Spirit in that little church drew me to my knees. God had taken a group of committed believers that had submitted to His authority and created an environment that is changing their community and culture.

When we become the kind of people God can use, understanding our identity in Christ and the kingdom of God, our relationship with Jesus affects every other relationship and area of life we come in contact with. We also become keenly aware of the spiritual warfare that exists and how we battle against it through the power of the Holy Spirit and God's Holy Word.

What kind of environment exists in the local church that you are a part of? Do you think of bricks, carpet, and nice chairs to sit in or do you see a people of God surrendered to His authority and direction? What kind of environment is God able to build through you? I never again noticed that church's open roof and mud floor—all I could see were God's people being obedient.

Scripture confirms Jesus' own prophecy about such heart-to-heart discipleship in John 14:12, *"I tell you the truth, anyone who has faith in me will do what I have been doing."* Spiritually transformed believers and their transformed churches are doing just what Jesus would be doing if He walked the earth today—pleasing and glorifying God.

No, I'm not saying you must have a church building with no roof and a mud floor to experience God's presence. God wants to transform lives in your church, too. He wants you and your church to follow the example of Jesus and live by sound principles rather than man-made programs, to-get lists, and to-do lists. He is waiting for you to get out of the wading pool of Christianity. He is waiting for you to jump in the deep end and totally immerse yourself in becoming like Jesus.

GET THIS ⇨ *The heart of this chapter…*
The core of spiritual transformation is a deep, abiding relationship with Jesus Christ. Transformational discipleship is helping people know and become like Christ. Your church can be a church that "gets it." Your church can glorify God with transformed believers worshiping God to-

gether, serving God, ministering to others, and pointing others to God by their obedience, love, and trust of Him.

GET PERSONAL ⇨ *How this applies to you and your church…*
List the times in your life when you have seen the kingdom of God reigning in the lives of the people around you. Stop and pray asking God to reign in your life, and for His reign in your life to be evident to those around you.

Will you take that leap of faith today and say…

• **YES!** I will acknowledge Jesus as the "main thing" and by doing so let Him empower all my other relationships.
• **YES!** I will answer the call of Jesus and follow Him wherever He leads me.
• **YES!** I will allow the Holy Spirit to empower me to become a servant leader.
• **YES!** I will use my lifestyle to express to the world how God is transforming my life.
• **YES!** I will make myself accountable to God for my attitudes, behavior, and relationships.
• **YES!** I will become flexible and adaptable to the many ways God will use to transform me and others into the likeness of Jesus.
• **YES!** I will become an intentional disciple of Jesus Christ and help others in their journeys to become like Him.
• **YES!**…God helping me: I will take my everyday, ordinary life—my sleeping, eating, going to work, and walking-around life—and place it before God as an offering. I won't become so well-adjusted to my culture that I fit into it without even thinking. Instead, I will fix my attention on God.
I'll be changed from the inside out…
I'll become Romans 12:1-2 on legs.
I'll will seek to become like Jesus and I will help others as they, too, seek to become like Him.

GET GOING ⇨ *Tips for proactive discipleship…*
1. Carefully read the following pages in this book to learn more about healthy churches, leadership teams, developing a discipleship ministry and ministry actions, discipleship needs, and resource tools to use.

2. Consider forming a spiritual transformation task force in your church to study this resource and to lead your church to experience spiritual transformation.

3. Every time you try an idea that helps or hinders your efforts to join God in spiritually transforming the lives of believers, send a summary of the idea to bsneed@lifeway.com so we can share it with others who are seeking to live the transformed life and are trying to lead others to do so.

4. For additional personal growth study *Jesus By Heart,* and *Experiencing God.*

TRANSFORMATIONAL DISCIPLESHIP. . .

Discipleship is a lifelong journey of obedience to Christ which transforms a person's values and behavior, and results in ministry in one's home, church, and the world.[24]

Discipleship is at the core of what the Christian church is about. Discipleship leads to evangelizing and changed lives, to righteous and abundant living, to joyful and meaningful service for all who desire it. Thus, what it's all about is this: **every believer is a disciple with a life-long potential of growth and service.**

Discipleship is learning to be like Christ. Knowing Christ, instead of just knowing about Him, results in a spiritual transformation in life and heart that reflects Christ to all we encounter. Since God's purpose is to save a dying world, and the only path to salvation is through His Son Jesus Christ, allowing the Holy Spirit to make Christ visible in us testifies of Christ's presence to the lost and believers alike.

Christ has said that believers are His body and, like Him, are to serve God's purpose. Since Jesus led by continuously pointing to the Father, believers are to do the same. Jesus is our model for leadership that serves God's eternal purpose. Therefore, **every believer, who would grow in Christlikeness is a leader, or potential leader, in pointing the way to God through Jesus Christ.**

Healthy Churches

Church health is a product of spiritually transformed people who are growing in obedience to their Master. Helping people know and become like Christ is the goal of transformational discipleship.

Our bodies use their various parts to inform us, strengthen us, and help us grow. Involvement with the rest of the body of Christ cannot happen in isolation. When we come together in groups of believers to study, pray, and fellowship, we encounter the Christ Who transforms us by the presence of His Holy Spirit in our lives and in our fellow believers.

Small groups usually make this encounter with the body easier to observe and participate in. (See pp. 86-88.) The added benefit is the growth of each member's understanding of how the body works. As the member is transformed, he becomes more aware of God at work in other groups, including, but not restricted to, his congregation. He can see the kingdom being grown when he encounters members of other congregations, denominations and ministries. He also sees how God moves across the bridges of relationship to form partnerships between groups.

To be a healthy church you must have a plan for discipling believers. While there are many ways a church can provide for discipleship, the method that works best for most churches is to have a ministry that focuses squarely on discipleship.

Diligent planning and faithful execution are musts for an effective discipleship ministry. Not only is planning required, it must be done regularly to be most effective. Not long ago churches planned a year in advance, then almost sat back and let those plans unfold. Today, planning is an ongoing discipline learning what God wants you to do, identifying where God is working, and joining Him as you plan for short- and long-term discipleship ministry.

The Leadership Team

In many churches, planning the discipleship ministry is led by a discipleship director who plans internally with discipleship leaders and externally with leaders of other areas of ministry in the church.

Selected discipleship leaders serve on the discipleship ministry leadership team. Together, team members plan and promote discipleship experiences, enlist leaders, and evaluate the effectiveness of the ministry. Members of the leadership team include the discipleship director, the pastor, and the church's educational staff. Beyond that, the team can in-

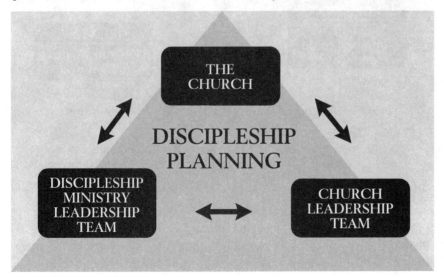

clude representatives who will champion a particular area of discipleship or special study.

Some churches find that having discipleship leaders as part of their Sunday School organization strengthens their discipleship ministry. Discipleship leaders can be a part of a Sunday School class or department, or both. Their work consists of identifying the discipleship needs of their class or department and planning discipleship experiences to meet those needs.

Some churches include the Sunday School director on the Discipleship leadership team, and the Discipleship director on the Sunday School council. This enables these two vital church ministries to be in a win-win situation, which means the church wins, too.

How to Develop a Discipleship Ministry

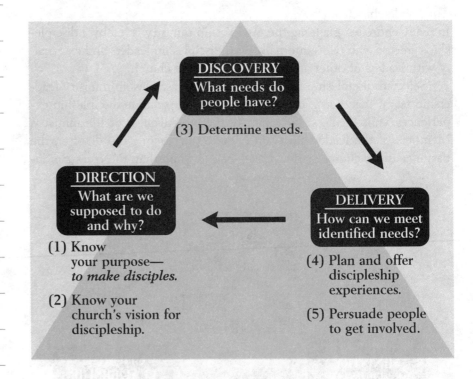

DISCOVERY
What needs do people have?

(3) Determine needs.

DIRECTION
What are we supposed to do and why?

(1) Know your purpose— *to make disciples.*

(2) Know your church's vision for discipleship.

DELIVERY
How can we meet identified needs?

(4) Plan and offer discipleship experiences.

(5) Persuade people to get involved.

(1) Know your purpose—*to make disciples.*
Planning incorporates all of the efforts that determine what an organization wants to be, where it is going, and how it will get there. Strategic

planning is a process that articulates organizational purpose (mission), weighs external opportunities and threats, gauges internal strengths and weaknesses, and determines appropriate goals and actions designed to shape the future. (See pp. 9-15.)

(2) Know your church's vision for discipleship.

Many churches are discovering the importance of thinking through and having a written vision statement. A vision statement (sometimes called a mission statement or a purpose statement) provides a focal point for identifying the reason for existence. A vision statement develops out of a common vision with which all people associated can identify. (See p. 84.) It is the pivot point upon which all the goals and actions are balanced.

Our vision statement at LifeWay Christian Resources is:

As God works through us we will help people and churches know Jesus Christ and seek His Kingdom by providing biblical solutions that spiritually transform individuals and cultures.

Sometimes trying to put your vision into words is harder than it seems. Consider appointing a task force to develop the statement. Members could include the pastor, education staff, and key people from Sunday School and discipleship ministries. Present it to the church body for approval. Including the church as a whole will insure a greater sense of ownership in the statement. After the church has developed its vision, encourage all areas of ministry to develop/adapt individual statements of vision or mission.

Planning with a Vision

Discipling believers is a vital part of every New Testament church. As you are thinking about a vision statement for a growing discipleship ministry consider the following questions:

- What is God calling us to do?
- Where are we now?
- What are our goals?
- How do we plan to get there?
- Who will be responsible?
- What resources do we need?

Discipleship Ministry Actions

A discipleship ministry can do many things for a church but it can't do everything. The following suggested ministry actions or objectives may provide a starting point as you define what you want your discipleship ministry to do.

Ministry Action 1
Assimilate new church members into the life of the church.
Through an effective ministry of discipleship, churches can help new Christians and other new members become part of the life of the church. This assimilation process is accomplished in many ways, and actually begins before a commitment to church membership. The key to assimilation is involvement that builds relationships and causes new members to bond with others in the church. (See p. 46). As people develop meaningful relationships, experience spiritual growth, and are involved in ministry, they will be assimilated into the life of the church.

Ministry Action 2
Guide disciples to grow in spiritual maturity.
An intentional, balanced, and effective discipleship ministry provides many opportunities for spiritual growth. Discipleship experiences that concentrate on Christian ethics, family life, spiritual gifts, skills for Christian living, and biblical doctrine help Christians develop spiritually. (See pp. 32-33.)

Ministry Action 3
Equip disciples to strengthen family relationships.
The first forum for discipleship is the home. Many churches are focusing their discipleship experiences on helping families strengthen their relationships and face crises together with Christian hope. (See p. 30.)

Ministry Action 4
Equip disciples for leadership and ministry.
Effective leadership and ministry is important to a church that is seeking to carry out the Great Commission. Servant leaders use their spiritual gifts to teach people, coordinate ministries, and equip others for ministry. The discipleship ministry of a church can equip Christians to become strong, biblical servant leaders. (See pp. 49, 55-56.)

People-groups

One way of approaching planning your discipleship ministry is to identify the people-groups in your church membership and in your community. People-groups represent categories of people who share life-situations with others. Each individual in a people-group is unique, but they share many of the same needs with others in the group. The most basic people-groups are *adults*, *youth*, *children*, and *preschoolers*.

Married couples is another example of a people-group. All married couples have some of the same needs, such as knowing how to communicate effectively with each other, learning to honor God in their marriage, and knowing how to show their love to each other. On the other hand, due to differences in the ages of couples and the length of time they have been married, the needs of some couples can differ from the needs of others.

There are two types of people-groups: *inside* people-groups and *outside* people-groups. Inside people-groups are those within your church, including church members and their families, and regular attenders. Outside people-groups are made up of people in your community who, though they don't belong to your church, are reachable for some of the discipleship experiences your church might offer.

Traditionally, discipleship ministries have ministered mainly to people-groups inside the church. But the discipleship and ministry needs of families, hurting people, and others can now be met effectively through discipleship experiences. For instance, a church in Indiana is reaching a large number of neighborhood children through TeamKID Clubs. Also, a church in Texas consistently reaches a large number of non-members through the many support groups it offers.

TeamKID Clubs, DiscipleNow youth events, parenting courses, marriage enrichment events, and support groups are but a few of the ways churches can minister to people outside the church. Churches with an outward focus are constantly seeking to meet the needs of all persons.

Knowing your people-groups is a good way to sharpen your focus. Your discipleship ministry can't do everything for everyone at all times, so this will help you determine where to put your time and energy.

People-Groups *Inside* the Church Who Need to Be Discipled

Adults
- Caregivers
- Church leadership
- College students
- Divorced
- Expectant mothers
- Grandparents
- Married couples
- Median adults
- Men
- Mothers working outside the home
- Newly married couples
- Parents of children
- Parents of preschoolers
- Parents of teenagers
- Retirees
- Senior adults
- Shift workers
- Single adults
- Single parents
- Stay-at-home moms
- Young adults
- Widows/widowers
- Women

Youth
- High school dropouts
- Junior high youth
- Middle school youth
- Pregnant teens
- Senior high youth
- Teenage parents

Children/Preschool
- Children of single parents
- Latchkey children
- Older children
- Older preschoolers
- Younger children
- Younger preschoolers

Multi-generational
- Abused
- Alcoholic
- Battered
- Bereaved
- Blended families
- Children of divorced parents
- Codependent
- Dysfunctional families
- Ethnic
- Families of people with AIDS
- Gifted
- Handicapped
- Hearing impaired
- Homebound
- Homeless
- Homosexuals
- Inactive church members
- Internationals
- Learning disabled
- New believers
- New church members
- Non-members who attend
- Overweight
- People with AIDS
- Substance/drug abusers
- Terminally ill
- Underweight
- Unemployed
- Visually impaired

People-Groups Outside the Church Who Need to Be Discipled

Many of the people-groups identified inside the church are the same as people-groups outside the church. Additional people-groups include:

• Church dropouts
• Families of nursing home residents
• Gang members
• Juvenile offenders
• Migrant workers
• Nursing home residents
• People in group homes
• People in prison
• Transient workers

After you have identified your people-groups you can begin looking at specific discipleship needs within each group.

(3) Determine needs.

What kinds of discipleship needs do believers have? Easy. Just think of yourself. What kinds of needs do you have? Do you need to know and use your spiritual gifts, develop a closer walk with God, become a more supportive parent or a more loving spouse? How about your devotional life; could it use a boost? Think of your own needs, and then multiply them a hundred-fold to begin to understand the scope of the discipleship needs of believers today.

Last year adults bought millions of self-help publications, attended thousands of special-interest workshops and seminars, and sought the help of an army of trained counselors, therapists, and mentors. Adults may not always know how to meet their needs, but they certainly are in touch with what those needs are.

This presents the church with a tremendous opportunity. Adults are searching for someone or something to help them make sense of their lives, find something to belong to, and learn how to make a contribution to their families and friends. Specifically, believers need to:

• know and use their spiritual gifts
• know and live out God's plan for their lives
• be able to share their faith with others
• develop a disciplined prayer life and Bible study

- strengthen relationships with family and friends
- involve themselves in ministry and service to others
- become involved in accountability groups
- build strong Christian families (adult believers)
- develop good parenting skills (adult believers)
- strengthen relationships with coworkers (adult believers)

A character-based discipleship ministry is designed to address needs and issues that other church ministries do not. Therefore, it can help believers deal with practical concerns that confront them every day of their lives. (See pp. 68-70.)

A discipleship ministry:
- teaches believers the disciplines that can lead to a spiritually transformed life in Christ.
- teaches believers how to pray, meditate, and worship; and to practice these disciplines daily.
- trains believers to share their faith with unsaved people and to build confidence as they witness on a regular basis.
- provides believers with opportunities for fellowship and the development of strong and lasting relationships with family, friends, and coworkers.
- equips believers to identify their spiritual gifts, choose a worthy ministry, and do ministry with compassion and competence.

Now that you have identified the people-groups you want to help and some specific discipleship needs within these groups, you're ready to look at ways to meet those needs.

(4) Plan and offer discipleship experiences.

Discipleship experiences are the heart of a discipleship ministry. Discipleship experiences are the actions churches take to meet people's discipleship needs. Some examples include: a short-term study of *Experiencing God* for adults or youth, a study of *Jesus on Leadership* for leaders, and a TeamKID Club for children or preschoolers. Discipleship experiences help people take important steps toward spiritual maturity and Christian ministry.

Most discipleship experiences today are modular in nature, which means they are not locked to any particular time in the weekly schedule. These experiences can be as effective on Sunday, Monday, or Wednesday night as Sunday or Tuesday morning. In one sense, this makes discipleship easier than ever to accomplish.

The challenge for today's discipleship leaders is to plan the appropriate discipleship experiences that meet people's needs, help transform lives, and enable the church to carry out its mission. It's a big challenge, but worth the effort!

An effective discipleship ministry includes an *adaptable, intentional, flexible,* and *ongoing* approach to identifying and meeting your church's discipleship needs. A comprehensive plan for discipling believers includes: training in spiritual growth, Christian doctrine, ethics, Christian history, how the church works, and ministry skills. (See pp 81-83.) Several approaches for meeting needs are available. The approaches used most often for discipling believers are:

- **Ongoing groups** in which the same core group of people meet together on a weekly basis.
- **Short-term groups** that study a variety of subjects. People belong to such a group only while a particular study is being conducted.
- **Support groups** which are formed to help people deal with personal or emotional needs in a confidential and supportive setting.
- **Individual study** which is used mostly by people who cannot or do not wish to participate in a group study.
- **Retreats** which are especially good for people wanting to learn a lot in a short period of time.

(5) Persuade people to get involved.
Now that you have a plan, you need leaders. Champions for discipleship make the most effective discipleship leaders. Discipleship champions:
- love God deeply.
- are growing in their relationship with God.
- want to see others' lives transformed.
- are gifted by God for the work they do.
- are patient, kind, and nonjudgmental.
- are committed to doing their best.
- enjoy working with people.
- have a positive attitude.
- are trainable and flexible.

Enlisting Leaders

Finding discipleship champions is a challenge. Make a list of persons who you feel would make good leaders. As you begin enlisting, make an appointment to meet with each person. Avoid enlisting someone while they are taking a drink from the water fountain in a hallway at church.

Take time to share the church's vision for discipleship ministry. Explain what is expected of each leader and review a job description if available for the position you're asking the person to take. Be open and honest. Provide a copy of the resource they would be using and tell what leadership training would be provided. Suggest that both of you take time to pray and set a time to get back together for an answer.

Training Leaders

When you enlist the very best, be sure to equip them to do their best. There is no substitute for trained, skilled, and spiritually transformed leaders. Leadership training opportunities include: individual study, mentoring by experienced leaders, and training courses provided in your church, association, and state. Every church leader needs to understand the concept of servant leadership as taught and practiced by Jesus. *Jesus on Leadership: Becoming a Servant Leader* is an excellent five-week study that helps people become true servant leaders.

Three video-driven courses for training discipleship leaders are *Serving God: Discovering and Using Your Spiritual Gifts, The 7 Laws of the Learner,* and *Teaching with Style. Serving God* helps leaders know and use their spiritual gifts. *The 7 Laws of the Learner* helps teachers improve their effectiveness as communicators and teach with life-changing impact. *Teaching with Style* shows how to put excitement, creativity, and flexibility into teaching.

The Christian Growth Study Plan (CGSP) provides a systematic approach to developing leaders who want to increase their knowledge and skills. The CGSP provides diploma plans for general and age-group discipleship leaders. Diploma requirements can be found in a *Christian Growth Study Plan Catalog,* available by calling (615) 251-2525.

Training conferences for discipleship and family ministry leaders are held each summer at Glorieta Conference Center in Glorieta, New Mexico and Ridgecrest Conference Center in Ridgecrest, North Carolina. **Discipleship and Family Week** is a week-long opportunity for discipleship ministry leadership training that is perfect for: pastors, ministers of education, associational leaders, church discipleship directors, and age-group discipleship directors. Special ministry track conferences include: ministries to children, family, men, preschoolers, seniors, singles, TeamKID, and women. Centrifuge and Summer Youth Celebration provide special conferences for teenagers. Additional track conferences include: Christian health, criminal justice, prayer ministry, and support groups. (For registration information, call toll free (800) 797-4222 for Glorieta and for Ridgecrest (800) 588-7222.)

Promoting Discipleship Experiences

There are numerous ways a discipleship ministry can be promoted and publicized, but none is as effective as transformed disciples. People who experience positive change in their lives through your transformational discipleship ministry are the best promoters you will ever have. However, promotion and publicity are still important. Effective publicity will pass the test of the three "C's" when it:

- Captures people's attention
- Communicates value, and
- Convinces people to participate.

A number of methods can be used to publicize discipleship experiences. Among them are: verbal and written announcements, newsletters and brochures, catalogs, posters, letters and cards, phone calls, personal encouragement, email, and Web pages on the Internet. Desktop publishing programs make it easy. You don't have to be a computer genius to turn out great-looking brochures, newsletters, and posters.

A church in California produces a catalog that describes the discipleship experiences it offers. A copy of the catalog is given to each church family along with an encouragement to participate. A church in Texas has its own Web site on the Internet. Among the information it provides is a list of available church-sponsored ministries, including discipleship experiences. A description of discipleship experiences and enrollment information can easily be provided on a Web site.

http://www.lifeway.com/discipleplus is a Web site brought to you by the LifeWay Discipleship and Family Adult Department. Check it out for the latest discipleship ministry information available from LifeWay.

RESOURCE TOOLS

Every believer begins as a spiritual infant. As disciples grow, they enter into an extended period of learning and development that lasts for a lifetime. As believers mature they find ways to express their spiritual gifts in ministry and leadership and their faith is multiplied in the lives of those they serve. The resources listed on the next few pages are divided into:
- beginning disciples
- developing disciples
- multiplying disciples

Resources in the following list are appropriate for different learning approaches that include:
- Individual study (I)
- Small-group study (SG)
- Large-group study (LG)
- Retreat (R)
- Guidance (G)
- Leadership training (LT)
- Magazine (MG)
- Study support (SS)
- Ongoing curriculum (O)

Resources are offered to assist you to find answers for your discipleship needs. Resources with separate leader guides are identified with u following the title. Many of the resources recommended for adults can also be adapted for use with college students. For a complete description of each resource, refer to a current *Church Materials Catalog*. If your church does not have a current catalog, you may call toll free (800) 458-2772 and request one.

BEGINNING DISCIPLES
Assimilating new believers into the life of the church.

Discipleship Need: To know the church's vision and commit to it.

Resources Adults	Approach	Sessions	Item No.
• *Basics for Baptists*	I, SG	8	0-7673-1901-X
• *Believe: Connecting Life & Faith*	MG		
• *How to Study Your Bible*	I, SG	11	0-7673-1915-X

• *Survival Kit: Five Keys to Effective Spiritual Growth*	I, SG	6	0-8054-9770-6
• *Survival Kit for New Christians, Basic English*	I, SG	11	0-8054-9683-1
• *Survival Kit for New Christians, Arabic Edition*	I, SG	11	0-7673-1911-7
• *Survival Kit for New Christians, Chinese Edition*	I, SG	11	0-7673-2380-7
• *Survival Kit for New Christians, Korean Edition*	I, SG	11	0-8054-9649-1
• *Survival Kit, How to Grow Spiritually, Spanish Ed*	I, SG	6	0-7673-3186-9
• *Taking the Next Step: A Guide for New Church Members* ◆	SG	4	0-8054-9442-1
• *Thine Is the Kingdom: The Reign of God in Today's World* ◆	I, SG	6	0-7673-3015-3
• *Thine Is the Kingdom, Leader Kit*	G, SS		0-7673-3018-8
• *Welcome to God's Family* (Tract)	I		0-7673-2783-7
• *Your Life and Your Church*	SG	7	0-7673-2005-0

Youth

• *Basic Church Stuff: A Guide for Assimilating New Youth Church Members*	LT		0-7673-2230-4
• *Survival Kit for Youth*	I, SG	11	0-8054-9602-5
• *Welcome to God's Family* (Tract)	I		0-7673-2783-7

Children

• *Now That I'm a Christian* ◆	I, SG	6	0-7673-2040-9
• *Survival Kit for New Christians, Children's Edition*	I, SG	6	0-8054-9601-7

Discipleship Need: To know and begin to use your spiritual gifts.

Resources	Approach	Sessions	Item No.
Adults			
• *Serving God: Discovering and Using Your Spiritual Gifts Kit*	G, SS	8	0-7673-2250-9
• *Spiritual Gifts: A Practical Guide to How God Works Through You* (Available 2/00)	I, SG	6	0-7673-9795-9
Youth			
• *How to Discover Your Spiritual Gifts*	R, SG	5	0-7673-1989-3

DEVELOPING DISCIPLES
Guiding disciples to grow in spiritual maturity.

Discipleship Need: To know how to make right choices.

Resources	Approach	Sessions	Item No.
Adults			
• *Christian Single*	MG		
• *Faithful and True: Sexual Integrity in a Fallen World*	SG	12	0-8054-9819-2
• *HomeLife*	MG		
• *Journey* (designed for women)	MG		
• *LifeAnswers: Making Sense of Your World*	I, SG	6	0-8054-9964-4
• *Living with Teenagers*	MG		
• *Mature Living*	MG		
• *Out of the Moral Maze* (designed for college)	SG	8	0-8054-9832-X
• *ParentLife*	MG		
• *Stand Firm* (designed for men)	MG		
• *Truth Matters...For You and Tomorrow's Generation* ◆	I, SG	8	0-8054-9834-6
Youth			
• *Holding Out for True Love*	R, SG	5	0-8054-9837-0
• *Make Up Your Mind*	R, SG	5	0-7673-33.28-4
• *Setting You Free to Make Right Choices* ◆	R, SG	8	0-8054-9828-1
• *Sexual Resolutions*	R, SG	5	0-6330-0289-5
• *The Youth Disciple* ◆	O, SG		
• *Tm4•1•2: It's Your Life* ◆	SG, LG	36	0-7673-3895-2
• *Tm4•1•2: Live It* ◆	SG, LG	36	0-7673-2991-0
• *True Love Waits Manual: Crossing Bridges with Purity*	G, SS		0-7673-9333-3
• *True Love Waits "The Gospel of Sex" Video Pak*	G, SG	3	0-7673-9195-0
• *Until You Say I Do*	R, SG	5	0-7673-3181-8
Children			
• *God's Way=My Way Activity Book for Grade 1* ◆	O, SG, LG	52	0-7673-9335-X
• *God's Way=My Way Activity Book for Grades 2-3* ◆	O, SG, LG	52	0-7673-9351-1
• *God's Way=My Way Activity Book for Grades 4-6* ◆	O, SG, LG	52	0-7673-9352-X
• *God's Way=My Way CD*	SS		0-6330-3967-5
• *God's Way=My Way Missions Video*	SS		0-7673-9359-7
• *TeamKID: Day-by-Day, Spanish Edition, Grades 1-3* ◆	O, SG, LG	36	0-7673-1982-6
• *TeamKID: Day-by-Day, Spanish Edition, Grades 4-6* ◆	O, SG, LG	36	0-7673-1983-4

• *Truth Works! Making Right Choices, Older Children* ◆	SG	8	0-8054-9830-3
• *Truth Works! Making Right Choices, Younger Children* ◆	SG	8	0-8054-9831-1

Preschoolers

• *God 'N Me Preschool TeamKID Activity Book* ◆	O, SG, LG	36	0--8054-9544-4
• *Here I Grow! Preschool TeamKID Activity Book* ◆	O, SG, LG	36	0-8054-9427-8
• *Way to Go! Preschool TeamKID Activity Book* ◆	O, SG, LG	36	0-7673-1992-3

Discipleship Need: To learn to live a distinctively Christian lifestyle.

Resources	Approach	Sessions	Item No.
Adults			
• *Christian Sex Education: Parent/Church Leader Guide*	LT		0-8054-9970-9
• *CrossSeekers: Transparent Living–Living a Life of Integrity*	SG (College)	6	0-7673-9296-5
• *CrossSeekers: Holy and Acceptable–Building a Pure Temple*	SG (College)	6	0-7673-9428-3
• *Destination: Principles for Making Life's Journey Count Leader Kit*	SG	4	0-7673-2603-2
• *Followology@Collegiate Ministry: Following Jesus in the Real World*	SG (College)	8	0-7673-9083-0
• *Heaven...A Place to Belong*	SG (College)	6	0-8054-9768-4
• *Heaven: Your Real Home*	I, SG	7	0-8054-9774-9
• *HomeLife*	MG		
• *Jesus by Heart: God Can Transform You to Be Like Jesus*	I, SG	6	0-7673-9851-3
• *Life in the Spirit* ◆	SG	12	0-7673-2586-9
• *Life in the Spirit, Leader Kit*	G, SS	12	0-7673-2648-2
• *Life in the Spirit, Weekend Manual*	LT	12	0-7673-3886-3
• *LifeAnswers: Making Sense of Your World*	I, SG	6	0-8054-9964-4
• *Living God's Word: Practical Lessons for Applying Scripture to Life*	SG	6	0-7673-2604-0
• *Living Your Christian Values*	I, SG	7	0-7673-9337-6
• *The Kingdom Agenda: Experiencing God in Your Workplace*	SG	6	0-7673-3408-6
• *The Man God Uses: Moved from the Ordinary to the Extraordinary*	I, SG	7	0-7673-3167-2
• *The Man God Uses, Leader Kit*	G, SS	7	0-7673-3183-4

- *MasterDesign: Your Calling as a Christian*   SG   6   0-7673-2671-7
- *MasterLife* ◆
  - *MasterLife 1: The Disciple's Cross*   SG   6   0-7673-2579-6
  - *MasterLife 2: The Disciple's Personality*   SG   6   0-7673-2580-X
  - *MasterLife 3: The Disciple's Victory*   SG   6   0-7673-2581-8
  - *MasterLife 4: The Disciple's Mission*   SG   6   0-7673-2582-6
  - *MasterLife Leader Kit*   G, SS   24   0-7673-2640-7
  - *MasterLife Weekend Manual*   LT   0-7673-3885-5
- *Search for Significance* ◆   I, SG   12   0-8054-9990-3
- *Seven Seasons of a Man's Life, Leader Kit*   G, SS   6   0-8054-9750-1
  - *The Season of Rebuilding*   SG   6   0-8054-9786-2
  - *The Seasons of Crisis and Renewal*   SG   6   0-8054-9787-0
  - *The Seasons of Reflection and Building*   SG   6   0-8054-9788-9
  - *The Seasons of Suffering and Success*   SG   6   0-8054-9785-4
- *The Mind of Christ* ◆   I, SG   12   0-8054-9870-2
- *The Mind of Christ, Leader Kit*   G, SS   12   0-7673-2625-3
- *Truth Matters...For You and Tomorrow's Generation*   I, SG   8   0-8054-9834-6

Youth

- *Heaven: Your Real Home, Youth Edition*   R, SG   8   0-8054-9778-1
- *Life in the Spirit, Youth Edition* ◆   I, SG   12   0-7673-2594-X
- *MasterLife, Youth Edition* ◆   SG   12   0-7673-3495-7
- *Relationship Revolution*   SG   7   0-7673-9868-8
- *Survival Kit for Youth*   I, SG   11   0-8054-9602-5
- *The Mind of Christ, Youth Edition* ◆   I, SG   12   0-7673-0000-9
- *The Notebook: A DiscipleYouth Experience* ◆   I, SG   13   0-7673-2231-2
- *The Search* ◆   SG   15   0-8054-9922-9
- *The Student God Uses*   R, SG   6   0-7673-9368-6
- *Tm4•1•2 It's Your Life! Student* ◆   O, SG, LG   36   0-7673-3895-2
- *WWJD? Student Interactive Edition*   R, SG   6   0-7673-3516-3

Children

- *Bible Buddies Activity Book for the New Testament* ◆   SG   26   0-7673-3453-1
- *Bible Buddies Activity Book for the Old Testament* ◆   SG   26   0-7673-3462-0
- *Bible Buddies Cassette Five-Pack*   SS   0-7673-3448-5
- *Boys and Girls – Alike and Different*   I   0-8054-9965-2
- *Children's Bible Drill Games and Activities, KJV*   SG   23   0-8054-9346-8
- *Children's Bible Drill Games and Activities, NIV*   SG   23   0-7673-3011-0
- *Children's Bible Drill Workbook, Cycle 1, KJV Edition*   I   0-7673-2028-X

Resource	Approach	Sessions	Item No.
• Children's Bible Drill Workbook, Cycle 1, NIV Edition	I		0-8054-9430-8
• Children's Bible Drill Cards, KJV, Cycle 1	SG		0-6330-0379-4
• Children's Bible Drill Cards, NIV, Cycle 1	SG		0-6330-0380-8
• Children's Bible Drill Leaders' and Judges' Guide	SS		0-7673-9130-6
• God's Way=My Way Activity Book for Grade 1 ◆	O, SG, LG	52	0-7673-9335-X
• God's Way=My Way Activity Book for Grades 2-3 ◆	O, SG, LG	52	0-7673-9351-1
• God's Way=My Way Activity Book for Grades 4-6 ◆	O, SG, LG	52	0-7673-9352-X
• God's Way=My Way CD	SS		0-6330-3967-5
• God's Way=My Way Missions Video	SS		0-7673-9359-7
• Learn-A-Verse: A Bible Skills Game	I		0-7673-2263-0
• My Body and Me	I		0-8054-9966-0
• Sex! What's That?	I		0-8054-9967-9
• TeamKID: Day-by-Day, Spanish Edition, Grades 1-3 ◆	O, SG, LG	36	0-7673-1982-6
• TeamKID: Day-by-Day, Spanish Edition, Grades 4-6 ◆	O, SG, LG	36	0-7673-1983-4

Preschoolers

Resource	Approach	Sessions	Item No.
• God 'N Me Preschool TeamKID Activity Book ◆	O, SG, LG	36	0--8054-9544-4
• Here I Grow! Preschool TeamKID Activity Book ◆	O, SG, LG	36	0-8054-9427-8
• Way to Go! Preschool TeamKID Activity Book ◆	O, SG, LG	36	0-7673-1992-3
• When I Go to Church: An Introduction to Congregational Worship for Preschoolers	I		0-7673-2024-7

Discipleship Need: To know and use their spiritual gifts.

Resources	Approach	Sessions	Item No.
Adults			
• Serving God: Discovering and Using Your Spiritual Gifts	SG	8	0-7673-2251-7
• Spiritual Gifts: A Practical Guide to How God Works Through You (Available 2/00)	SG	6	0-7673-9795-9
Youth			
• How to Discover Your Spiritual Gifts	R, SG	5	0-7673-1989-3

Discipleship Need: To know and do God's will.

Resources	Approach	Sessions	Item No.
Adults			
• CrossSeekers: Discipleship Covenant for New Generation	SG	9	0-7673-9084-9
• CrossSeekers: Spiritual Intimacy–Drawing Closer to God	SG	6	0-7673-9427-5

Resource	Approach	Sessions	Item No.
• Experiencing God: Knowing and Doing the Will of God	SG	12	0-8054-9954-7
• Fresh Encounter: God's Pattern for Revival and Spiritual Awakening	SG	6	0-8054-9920-2
• Fresh Encounter: A Plumb Line for God's People	SG	6	0-8054-9919-9
• God's Invitation: A Challenge to College Students	I, SG	7	0-8054-9679-3
• Seven Realities of Experiencing God, Video Series	I, SG	6	0-8054-9853-2
• When God Speaks: How to Recognize God's Voice and Respond in Obedience	I, SG	7	0-8054-9822-2

Youth

Resource	Approach	Sessions	Item No.
• Experiencing God, Youth Edition ◆	I, SG	9	0-8054-9925-3
• Experiencing God, Youth Video Series	SS	9	0-8054-9839-7
• Experiencing God, Youth Edition Spanish ◆	I, SG	9	0-8054-9845-1
• Lift High the Torch: An Invitation to Experiencing God	R, SG	4	0-8054-9847-8
• The Student God Uses	SG	6	0-7673-9368-6
• When God Speaks, Youth Edition	R, SG	7	0-7673-2592-3

Children

Resource	Approach	Sessions	Item No.
• Experiencing God, Preteen Edition ◆	SG	9	0-8054-9859-1
• Experiencing God Preteen Edition, Spanish ◆	SG	9	0-8054-9850-8

Discipleship Need: To be able to share their faith with others.

Resources	Approach	Sessions	Item No.
Adults			
• CrossSeekers: Fearless–Sharing an Authentic Witness	SG	6	0-7673-9865-3
• How to Have a Full and Meaningful Life	I		0-7673-2785-3
• Into Their Shoes: Helping the Lost Find Christ ◆	SG	6	0-8054-9769-2
• Learning to Share My Faith	SG	6	0-8054-9864-8
• Meeting Needs: Sharing Christ: Ministry Evangelism ◆	SG	6	0-8054-9840-0
• Meeting Needs: Sharing Christ, Leader Kit	G, SS		0-8054-9838-9
• Share Jesus Without Fear ◆	SG	4	0-7673-3059-5
• Share Jesus Without Fear Kit	G, SS	4	0-7673-3057-9
• Witnessing Through Your Relationships ◆	SG	13	0-8054-9893-1

Youth

Resource	Approach	Sessions	Item No.
• The Notebook: A DiscipleYouth Experience ◆	I, SG	13	0-7673-2231-2
• Share Jesus Without Fear: Students Reaching Students	R, SG	5	0-7673-3820-0

Discipleship Need: To understand biblical doctrines and teachings.

Resources	Approach	Sessions	Item No.
Adults			
• *A Heart Like His: Seeking the Heart of God Through a Study of David*	SG	10	0-7673-2596-6
• *A Heart Like His, Leader Kit*	SS		0-7673-2653-9
• *A Heart Like His, Audiotapes*	SS	10	0-7673-2652-0
• *A Woman's Heart: God's Dwelling Place* ◆	SG	10	0-8054-9836-2
• *A Woman's Heart, Leader Kit*	G, SS	10	0-8054-9826-5
• *A Woman's Heart, Audiotapes*	SS	10	0-8054-9797-8
• *Life Lessons from Women in the Bible*	I, SG	6	0-7673-3574-0
• *Baptist Adults*	MG		
• *The Baptist Faith and Message*	SG	5	0-8054-9597-5
• *The Baptist Faith and Message, Teaching Workbook*	I, SG	5	0-8054-9411-1
• *Basics for Baptists*	I, SG	8	0-7673-1901-X
• *Foundations of the Faith: The Doctrines Baptists Believe* ◆	I, SG	6	0-7673-3277-6
• *Living Beyond Yourself: Exploring the Fruit of the Spirit*	I, SG	11	0-7673-9275-2
• *Our Christian Hope: Bible Answers to Questions About the Future* ◆	I, SG	6	0-7673-3477-9
• *Our Christian Hope, Leader Kit*	G, SS	6	0-7673-3483-3
• *Partners with God: Bible Truths About Giving*	I, SG	6	0-7673-2095-6
• *Step by Step Through the New Testament*	SG	13	0-8054-9946-6
• *Step by Step Through the Old Testament*	SG	13	0-7673-2619-9
• *Thine Is the Kingdom: The Reign of God in Today's World*	SG	6	0-7673-3015-3
• *To Live Is Christ: The Life and Ministry of Paul* ◆	SG	11	0-7673-3412-4
• *To Live Is Christ, Leader Kit*	G, SS	11	0-7673-3402-7
• *To Live Is Christ, Audiotapes*	SS	11	0-7673-2995-3
Youth			
• *Survival Kit for Youth*	I, SG	11	0-8054-9602-5
• *Truths That Make a Difference*	SG	5	0-8054-9594-0
• *The Youth Disciple*	MG		
Children			
• *Bible Buddies Activity Book for the New Testament* ◆	SG	26	0-7673-3453-1
• *Bible Buddies Activity Book for the Old Testament* ◆	SG	26	0-7673-3462-0
• *Bible Buddies Cassette Five-Pack*	SS		0-7673-3448-5

• *Boys and Girls – Alike and Different*	I		0-8054-9965-2
• *Children's Bible Drill Games and Activities, KJV*	SG	23	0-8054-9346-8
• *Children's Bible Drill Games and Activities, NIV*	SG	23	0-7673-3011-0
• *Children's Bible Drill Workbook, Cycle 1, KJV Edition*	I		0-7673-2028-X
• *Children's Bible Drill Workbook, Cycle 1, NIV Edition*	I		0-8054-9430-8
• *Children's Bible Drill Cards, KJV, Cycle 1*	SG		0-6330-0379-4
• *Children's Bible Drill Cards, NIV, Cycle 1*	SG		0-6330-0380-8
• *Children's Bible Drill Leaders' and Judges' Guide*	SS		0-7673-9130-6
• *God Is In Charge (Grades 1-3)*	SS	5	0-7673-2106-5
• *God's Plan: Now and Forever (Grades 4-6)*	SG	5	0-7673-2103-0
• *Jesus Loves Me, Too (Grades 1-3)*	SG	5	0-7673-2105-7
• *Jesus, My Savior (Grades 4-6)*	SG	5	0-7673-2102-2
• *Learn-A-Verse: A Bible Skills Game*	I		0-7673-2263-0
• *Stuff: Using All God Has Given Me (Grades 1-6)* ◆	SG	5	0-7673-2107-3

Preschoolers

• *God's Plan for Me*	SG	5	0-7673-2109-X
• *I Learn About Jesus*	SG	5	0-7673-2108-1

Discipleship Need: To develop a disciplined prayer and devotional life.

Resources	Approach	Sessions	Item No.
Adults			
• *A House of Prayer: Prayer Ministries in Your Church* (Available 12/99)	LT		0-7673-9393-7
• *Day-by-Day in God's Kingdom: A Discipleship Journal*	I, SG		0-7673-2577-X
• *Disciple's Prayer Life: Walking in Fellowship with God*	SG	12	0-7673-3494-9
• *The Doctrine of Prayer*	I, SG	5	0-7673-1919-2
• *In God's Presence: Daily Guide to a Meaningful Prayer Life*	SG	6	0-8054-9900-8
• *Journey*	MG		
• *Living God's Word: Lessons for Applying Scripture to Life*	SG	6	0-7673-2604-0
• *Prayer in the Family: A Home Activity Book*	I, Family		0-7673-3924-X
• *Stand Firm*	MG		
• *The Vision of His Glory*	SG	12	0-7673-9116-0
• *The Vision of His Glory Leader Kit*	G, SS		0-7673-9176-4
• *Watchman Prayer Guide* ◆	I, SG		0-8054-9962-8
• *Watchman Prayer Ministry Planning Kit*	LT		0-8054-9960-1
• *Whispers of Hope*	I		0-7673-9278-7

Youth

Resource	Approach	Sessions	Item No.
• *An Awesome Way to Pray Journal* ◆	I		0-7673-9086-5
• *Circle Your World with Prayer*	R, SG	5	0-7673-9355-4
• *Deepening Discipleship*	R, SG	5	0-7673-3180-X
• *DiscipleHelps: A Daily Quiet Time Guide and Journal*	I		0-8054-9451-0
• *In God's Presence, Youth Edition*	I, SG	6	0-7673-0001-7
• *Prayer in the Family: A Home Activity Book*	I Family		0-7673-3924-X
• *Survival Kit for Youth*	I, SG	11	0-8054-9602-5
• *When God Speaks, Youth Edition*	R, SG	6	0-7673-2592-3

Children

Resource	Approach	Sessions	Item No.
• *Prayer in the Family: A Home Activity Book*	I, Family		0-7673-3924-X
• *Survival Kit for New Christians, Children's Edition*	I, SG	6	0-8054-9601-7

Discipleship Need: To develop positive skills for parenting and grandparenting.

Resources	Approach	Sessions	Item No.
Adults			
• *Empowered Parenting: Raising Kids in the Nurture and Instruction of the Lord*	SG	8	0-8054-9815-X
• *Five Love Languages of Children, Parent Activity Guide*	I, SG		0-7673-3898-7
• *Five Love Languages of Children, Video Pack*	G, SS		0-7673-3899-5
• *Grandparenting by Grace*	SG	12	0-8054-9897-4
• *HomeLife*	MG		
• *Living with Teenagers*	MG		
• *Mature Living*	MG		
• *New Faces in the Frame: Guide to Marriage & Parenting in Blended Families*	I, SG	12	0-8054-9817-6
• *Parenting by Grace Parent Guide*	SG	10	0-8054-9939-3
• *ParentLife*	MG		
• *Shaping the Next Generation*	I, SG	7	0-7673-3476-0
• *Shaping the Next Generation, Leader Kit*	G, SS	7	0-7673-3484-1
• *Building Strong Families* (appropriate for youth also)			
○ *Kindness in the Family: A Home Activity Book*	I, Family		0-7673-3174-5
○ *Peace in the Family: A Home Activity Book*	I, Family		0-7673-2584-2
○ *Prayer in the Family: A Home Activity Book*	I, Family		0-7673-3924-X
○ *Self-Control in the Family: A Home Activity Book*	I, Family		0-7673-3175-3

Discipleship Need: To strengthen relationships with husband-wife, family, and friends.

Resources	Approach	Sessions	Item No.
Adults			
• *Building Relationships: A Discipleship Guide for Married Couples* ◆	SG	12	0-8054-9855-9
• *Building Strong Families*	SG		0-8054-6370-4
• *Communication and Intimacy: Covenant Marriage Couple Guide* ◆	SG	12	0-7673-9459-3
• *Counsel for the Nearly and Newly Married, Couple Guide* ◆	SG	8	0-8054-9610-6
• *Covenant Marriage: Partnership and Commitment* ◆	SG	12	0-7673-9458-5
• *CrossSeekers: Soul Food for Relationships*	I, SG	6	0-7673-9426-7
• *Five Love Languages Video Pack*	I, SG	2	0-8054-9862-1
• *Five Love Languages of Children, Parent Activity Guide*	I, SG		0-7673-3898-7
• *Five Love Languages of Children, Video Pack*	G, SS		0-7673-3899-5
• *HomeLife*	MG		
• *HomeLife's TODAY* (magazine for unchurched families)	I		
• *Making Love Last Forever* ◆	SG	12	0-8054-9791-9
• *New Faces in the Frame: A Guide to Marriage and Parenting in the Blended Family*	SG	12	0-8054-9817-6
Youth			
• *Holding Out for True Love*	R, SG	5	0-8054-9837-0
• *How to Help Your Friends*	R, SG		
• *Relationship Revolution*	R, SG	6	0-7673-9868-8
• *Sexual Resolutions*	R, SG	5	0-6330-0289-5
• *Sexuality: God's Gift*	R, SG	4	0-8054-9968-7
• *Until You Say I Do*	R, SG	5	0-7673-3181-8
• *Your Circle of Friends*	R, SG	5	0-7673-9073-3
Children			
• *KidShare: What Do I Do Now? Helping Children Deal with Divorce* ◆	SG	13	0-8054-9887-7
• *Kindness in the Family: A Home Activity Book*	I, Family		0-7673-3174-5
• *Peace in the Family: A Home Activity Book*	I, Family		0-7673-2584-2
• *Prayer in the Family: A Home Activity Book*	I, Family		0-7673-3924-X
• *Self-Control in the Family: A Home Activity Book*	I, Family		0-7673-3175-3

Discipleship Need: To overcome negative behavior and lifestyle choices.

Resources	Approach	Sessions	Item No.
Adults			
• *A Time for Healing: Coming to Terms with Your Divorce* ◆	SG	6	0-8054-9875-3
• *Breaking the Cycle of Hurtful Family Experiences* ◆	SG	12	0-8054-9981-4
• *Choosing to Change: The First Place Challenge*	SG	10	
• *Christian Single*	MG		
• *Conquering Chemical Dependency* ◆	SG	12	0-8054-9983-0
• *Conquering Codependency* ◆	SG	12	0-8054-9975-X
• *Conquering Eating Disorders* ◆	SG	12	0-8054-9977-6
• *Discovering the Winning Edge* (College)	SG	5	0-7673-3178-8
• *Faithful and True: Sexual Integrity in a Fallen World*	SG	12	0-8054-9819-2
• *First Place: A Christ-Centered Health Program* ◆			
○ *First Place Favorites*	SS		0-7673-2616-4
○ *First Place: Member Notebook*	SG	10	0-7673-2609-1
○ *First Place Bible Studies*			
○ *Everyday Victory for Everyday People*	SG	10	0-8054-9994-6
○ *Giving Christ First Place*	SG	10	0-8054-9995-4
○ *Life That Wins*	SG	10	0-8054-9993-8
○ *Living the Legacy*	SG	10	0-7673-3572-4
○ *Pressing On to the Prize*	SG	10	0-8054-9775-7
• *HomeLife*	MG		
• *Journey*	MG		
• *Living with Teenagers*	MG		
• *Making Peace with Your Past* ◆	SG	12	0-8054-9986-5
• *Mature Living*	MG		
• *Moving Beyond Your Past* ◆	SG	12	0-8054-9927-X
• *ParentLife*	SG		
• *Quitting for Good: A Christ-Centered Approach to Nicotine Dependency* ◆	SG	9	0-8054-9844-3
• *Recovering from the Losses of Life*	SG	9	
• *Shelter from the Storm: Hope for Survivors of Sexual Abuse* ◆	SG	12	0-8054-9979-2
• *Stand Firm*	MG		
• *Strength for the Journey: A Biblical Perspective on Discouragement and Depression*	I, SG	9	0-7673-9105-5
• *Untangling Relationships: A Christian Perspective on Codependency* ◆	SG	12	0-8054-9973-3

Youth

• *First Place, Youth Edition, Leader Guide*	LT		0-7673-3071-4
• *First Place, Youth Edition: Encounters With God*	SG	8	0-7673-3069-2
• *First Place, Youth Edition: Life of Jesus*	SG	8	0-7673-3091-9
• *First Place, Youth Edition: Meal Planner*	SG		0-7673-3072-2
• *Fake Answers*	R, SG	13	0-7673-2031-X
• *Killers: Alcohol and Other Drugs, Member* ◆	SG	13	0-8054-9884-2
• *The Search, Member* ◆	SG	6	0-8054-9922-9
• *Untangling Relationships, Youth Edition* ◆	SG	12	0-8054-9848-6
• *Winning in the Land of Giants*	R, SG	6	0-7673-2605-9

MULTIPLYING DISCIPLES
Equipping disciples for leadership and ministry.

Discipleship Need: To develop the mind and attitude of a servant.

Resources	Approach	Sessions	Item No.
Adults			
• *Jesus on Leadership: Developing Servant Leaders* ◆	I, SG	6	0-7673-9855-6
• *Jesus on Leadership: Developing Servant Leaders Kit*	G, SS	6	0-8054-9351-4
• *Jesus on Leadership, Spanish Edition*	I, SG	6	0-7673-2668-7
Youth			
• *Deepening Discipleship*	R, SG	5	0-7673-3180-X
• *How to Help Your Friends*	R, SG	5	0-8054-9426-X
• *Jesus on Leadership, Student Edition* ◆ (Available 12/99)	I, SG	6	0-7673-9487-9
• *The Mind of Christ, Youth Edition* ◆	I, SG	12	0-7673-0000-9

Discipleship Need: To develop skills and know how to serve effectively in a chosen ministry.

Resources	Approach	Sessions	Item No.
Adults			
• *Christian Single*	MG		
• *DecisionTime: Commitment Counseling*	LT	13	0-7673-9179-9
• *Forward Together: A New Vision for Sr-Adult Ministry*	I, SG	4	0-7673-3115-X
• *HomeLife*	MG		
• *Journey*	MG		
• *Leading Criminal Justice Ministry: Bringing Shalom*	LT		0-7673-9114-4

Title	Type	#	ISBN
• Leading Family Ministry in a Church	LT		0-7673-3407-8
• LIFE Support Group Series Training Video	LT		0-8054-9881-8
• Living with Teenagers	MG		
• MasterLife ◆			
○ MasterLife 1: The Disciple's Cross	SG	6	0-7673-2579-6
○ MasterLife 2: The Disciple's Personality	SG	6	0-7673-2580-X
○ MasterLife 3: The Disciple's Victory	SG	6	0-7673-2581-8
○ MasterLife 4: The Disciple's Mission	SG	6	0-7673-2582-6
○ MasterLife Leader Kit	LT	24	0-7673-2640-7
○ MasterLife Weekend Manual	LT		0-7673-3885-5
• Mature Living	MG		
• Meeting Needs, Sharing Christ			
○ Ministry Evangelism, Kit	G, SS	6	0-8054-9838-9
○ Meeting Needs, Sharing Christ: Ministry Evangelism ◆	SG	6	0-8054-9840-0
○ Meeting Needs, Sharing Christ, Audiotapes	SS	6	0-7673-2639-3
○ Meeting Needs, Sharing Christ, Video	SS		0-8054-9806-0
• Men's Ministry Manual	LT		
• ParentLife	MG		
• Serving God: Discovering and Using Your Spiritual Gifts	I, SG	8	0-7673-2251-7
• Serving God: Discovering Using Spiritual Gifts Kit	G, SS	8	0-7673-2250-9
• Single Adult Ministry Solution, The	I, SG	6	
• Spiritual Gifts: A Practical Guide to How God Works Through You (Available 2/00)	SG	6	0-7673-9795-9
• Stand Firm	MG		
• Start a Revolution: Nine World-Changing Strategies for Single Adults	I, SG	8	0-8054-9823-0
• Teaching with Style	I, SG	6	0-7673-1985-0
• Teaching with Style, Video Kit	G, SS		0-7673-1986-9
• Transformational Discipleship: Your Church Helping People Be Like Jesus	LT		0-7673-9850-5
• Vision, Variety, and Vitality	I, SG	4	0-8054-9440-5
• WiseCounsel: Skills for Lay Counseling ◆	SG	13	0-7673-2615-6
• WiseCounsel Video	SS		0-8054-8399-3
• Women Reaching Women: Beginning and Building a Growing Women's Enrichment Ministry	LT		0-7673-2593-1
• 7 Laws of the Learner	LT	7	0-7673-1979-6
• 7 Laws of the Learner Video Kit	G, SS		0-7673-1980-X

[24]Pages 96-121 are adapted from Leading Discipleship in a Church 1998-99. Roy Edgemon and Steve Williams (Nashville: Convention Press, 1998) 5-64.

STATE DISCIPLESHIP OFFICES

Alabama
(334) 288-2460
P. O. Box 11870
Montgomery, AL 36111-0870

Alaska
(907) 344-9627
1750 O'Malley Road
Anchorage, AK 99516-1371

Arizona
(602) 240-3280
Suite 550
4520 N. Central Avenue
Phoenix, AZ 85012-1835

Arkansas
(501) 376-4791
P. O. Box 552
Little Rock, AR 72203-0552

California
(209) 229-9533
678 East Shaw Avenue
Fresno, CA 93710-7779

Canada
(403) 932-5688
Postal Bag 300
Cochrane, Alberta
CANADA TOL OWO

Colorado
(303) 771-2480
7393 S. Alton Way
Englewood, CO 80112-2372

Dakotas
(701) 255-3765
P. O. Box 7187
Bismarck, ND 58507-7187

District of Columbia
(202) 265-1526
1628 Sixteenth Street, NW
Washington, DC 20009-3099

Florida
(904) 396-2351
1230 Hendricks Avenue
Jacksonville, FL 32207-8696

Georgia
(770) 455-0404
2930 Flowers Road, South
Atlanta, GA 30341-5562

Hawaii
(808) 946-9581
2042 Vancouver Drive
Honolulu, HI 96822-2491

Illinois
(217) 786-2600
P. O. Box 19247
Springfield, IL 62794-9247

Indiana
(317) 241-9317
P. O. Box 24189
Indianapolis, IN 46224-0189

Iowa
(515) 278-1566
2400 86th Street, Suite 27
Des Moines, IA 50322-4331

Kansas-Nebraska
(785) 273-4880
5410 Southwest Seventh
Topeka, KS 66606-2398

Kentucky
(502) 245-4101
P. O. Box 43433
Louisville, KY 40253-0433

Louisiana
(318) 448-3402
P. O. Box 311
Alexandra, LA 71309-0311

Maryland/Delaware
(410) 290-5290
10255 Old Columbia Road
Columbia, MD 21046-1736

Michigan
(248) 577-4200
15635 West Twelve Mile Road
Southfield, MI 48076-3091

Minnesota/Wisconsin
(507) 282-3636
519 16th Street, S. E.
Rochester, MN 55904-5296

Mississippi
(601) 968-3800
P. O. Box 530
Jackson, MS 39205-0530

Missouri
(573) 635-7931
400 East High Street
Jefferson City, MO 65101-3215

Montana
(406) 252-7537
P. O. Box 99
Billings, MT 59103-0099

Nevada
(702) 786-0406
406 California Avenue
Reno, NV 89509-1520

New England
(508) 393-6013
5 Oak Avenue
Northborough, MA
01532-1723

New Mexico
(505) 924-2300
P. O. Box 485
Albuquerque, NM 87103-0485

New York
(315) 433-1001
6538 Collamer Road
East Syracuse, NY 13057-1013

North Carolina
(919) 467-5100
P. O. Box 1127
Cary, NC 27512-1107

Northwest
(360) 882-2100
3200 N. E., 109th Avenue
Vancouver, WA 98682-7749

Ohio
(614) 258-8491
1680 East Broad Street
Columbus, OH 43203-2095

Oklahoma
(405) 942-3800
3800 N. May Avenue
Oklahoma City, OK
73112-6506

Pennsylvania-South Jersey
(717) 652-5856
4620 Fritchey Street
Harrisburg, PA 17109-2895

South Carolina
(803) 765-0030
190 Stoneridge Drive
Columbia, SC 29210-8239

Tennessee
(615) 373-2255
P. O. Box 728
Brentwood, TN 37024-0728

Texas
(214) 828-5100
333 North Washington
Dallas, TX 75246-1798

Utah-Idaho
(801) 572-5350
P. O. Box 1347
Draper, UT 84020-1347

Virginia
(804) 672-2100
P. O. Box 8568
Richmond, VA 23226

West Virginia
(304) 757-0944
One Mission Way
Scott Depot, WV 25560-9406

Wyoming
(307) 472-4087
P. O. Box 4779
Casper, WY 82604

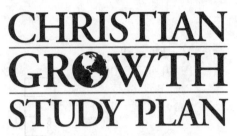

CHRISTIAN GROWTH STUDY PLAN

Preparing Christians to Serve

In the Christian Growth Study Plan *Transformational Discipleship: Your Church Helping People Be Like Jesus*, is a resource for course credit in seven diploma plans. To receive credit, read the book, summarize the chapters, show your work to your pastor, a staff member, or church leader, then complete the information on page 125.

Send completed page 125 to the Christian Growth Study Plan, 127 Ninth Avenue North, Nashville, TN 37234-0117. Fax: 615-251-5067. Page 125 may be duplicated. For information about the Christian Growth Study Plan, refer to the current *Christian Growth Study Plan Catalog*. Your church office may have a copy. If not, request a free copy by calling 615-251-2525.

Course Credit Information for
Transformational Discipleship: Your Church Helping People Be Like Jesus

You will receive course credit toward the diploma designed for your position(s).

LS-0016 (Preschool Discipleship Training)
LS-0021 (Children's Discipleship Training)
LS-0034 (Adult Discipleship Training)
LS-0048 (Discipleship Training General
       Church Leader)

LS-0034 (Family Enrichment Leader)
LS-0067 (Associational Discipleship Training)
LS-0091 (Church Leadership)

Transformational Discipleship: Your Church Helping People Be Like Jesus

☐ LS-0016 (Preschool Discipleship Training)
☐ LS-0021 (Children's Discipleship Training)
☐ LS-0034 (Adult Discipleship Training)
☐ LS-0048 (Discipleship Training General
              Church Leader)

☐ LS-0034 (Family Enrichment Leader)
☐ LS-0067 (Associational Discipleship Training)
☐ LS-0091 (Church Leadership)

PARTICIPANT INFORMATION

Social Security Number (USA ONLY)

Personal CGSP Number*

Home Phone

Date of Birth (MONTH, DAY, YEAR)

Name (First, Middle, Last)

Address (Street, Route, or P.O. Box)

City, State, or Province

Zip/Postal Code

CHURCH INFORMATION

Church Name

Address (Street, Route, or P.O. Box)

City, State, or Province

Zip/Postal Code

CHANGE REQUEST ONLY

☐ Former Name

☐ Former Address

City, State, or Province

Zip/Postal Code

☐ Former Church

City, State, or Province

Zip/Postal Code

Signature of Pastor, Conference Leader, or Other Church Leader

Date

*New participants are requested but not required to give SS# and date of birth. Existing participants, please give CGSP# when using SS# for the first time. Thereafter, only one ID# is required. **Mail to:** Christian Growth Study Plan, 127 Ninth Ave., North, Nashville, TN 37234-0117. Fax: (615)251-5067

Rev. 6-99

125

NOTES

NOTES

NOTES